THE AMERICAN KENNEL CLUB'S

Train Your Puppy Right

AN OFFICIAL PUBLICATION OF THE

AMERICAN
KENNEL CLUB

Lead Editor: Amy Deputato
Copyeditor: Karen Julian
Consulting Editors: Babette Haggerty and Andrew DePrisco
Art Director: Cindy Kassebaum
Production Manager: Laurie Panaggio
Production Supervisor: Jessica Jaensch
Production Coordinator: Leah Rosalez
Book Project Specialist: Karen Julian

Vice President, Chief Content Officer: June Kikuchi
Vice President, Kennel Club Books: Andrew DePrisco
BowTie Press: Jennifer Calvert, Amy Deputato, Karen Julian, Jarelle S. Stein

American Kennel Club: Cynthia Beagles, Mary Burch, Aliza Burns, Gina DiNardo, Rebecca Mercer, Lisa Peterson, Daphna Straus, Dennis B. Sprung

Photographs by: ©AKC/Russell Bianca: 4; ©AKC/Lisa Croft-Elliott: 137; Alamy: 10; Gina Cioli/ BowTie Studio: title page, 6, 14, 54, 56, 103; Mary Anne Coleman: 87 (bottom); Carolyn C. Corbett: 86 (bottom right); Penny DiLoreto (Puppies Dot Com): 87 (top); Shirley Fernandez (Fox Hill Photo): 11; Isabelle Francais: 7, 13, 18, 23, 25, 27, 29, 30, 31, 23, 33, 34, 35, 37, 41, 42, 53, 70, 72, 80, 81, 90, 91, 92, 98, 111, 122, 126, 129, 131, 141, 146, 149, 150; Tammy Hagen: 86 (bottom left); Jane Hufstader: 86 (top); Daniel Johnson (Fox Hill Photo): 44, 65, 71. 76, 78, 102, 106, 107, 119, 121, 123, 124, 127; Paulette Johnson (Fox Hill Photo): 58, 108, 117; Mark Raycroft: 9, 43, 63, 101, 133, 135, 138; Jerry Shulman: 66; Shutterstock: cover, cover inset, back cover (both), contents page, 8, 12, 16, 19, 20, 21, 22, 24, 38, 40, 45, 46, 48, 49, 50, 52, 57, 61, 62, 64, 67, 68, 73, 74, 75, 77, 85, 88, 93, 96, 97, 100, 110, 112, 113, 114, 116, 118, 130, 132, 134, 136, 142, 143, 144, 145, 148, 151; Connie Summers (Fox Hill Photo): 55; Connie Summers and Paulette Johnson (Fox Hill Photo): 83, 89, 95, 128

BowTie Press
A Division of BowTie, Inc.
3 Burroughs, Irvine, CA 92618, USA
www.bowtiepress.com

Library of Congress Cataloging-in-Publication Data

The American Kennel Club's train your puppy right.
     p. cm.
  Includes bibliographical references and index.
  ISBN 978-1-935484-90-5
  1. Puppies--Training. I. American Kennel Club.
  SF431.A4364 2012
  636.7'07--dc23
                        2012009035

Printed and bound in the United States
15 14 13 12   1 2 3 4 5 6 7 8 9 10

Contents

AKC President and CEO Dennis B. Sprung and Pomeranian Blue Moon's Back in the USSR, RN ("Lennon").

AMERICAN KENNEL CLUB®

Dennis B. Sprung
President and
Chief Executive Officer

Welcome to *The American Kennel Club's Train Your Puppy Right*. Whether you're a longtime dog owner or you've just gotten your very first puppy, we wish you a lifetime of happiness and enjoyment with your new pet.

In this book, you'll learn about all the fun things you can do with your new dog. The American Kennel Club believes that this book will serve as a useful guide on the lifelong journey you'll take with your canine companion.

Need help with house-training? Want to prevent chewed furniture? Trying to keep your new puppy from jumping on your houseguests? *Train Your Puppy Right* will provide the training tips and socialization skills that will get your dog off to a good start.

We also encourage you to find an AKC club that offers training classes in your area. Many AKC clubs offer classes, ranging from AKC S.T.A.R. Puppy to competitive obedience and agility; you can find clubs at www.akc.org/events/trainingclubs.cfm.

Once you've started training, why not try an AKC event? There is something for all dogs and owners, including AKC Rally®, obedience, agility, conformation (dog shows), hunt tests, field trials, and more. Plus, tens of thousands of dogs earn Canine Good Citizen® certification each year by demonstrating their good manners at home and in the community. We invite you and your puppy to become involved in AKC events, too! Learn how at www.akc.org/events.

Finally, we encourage you to connect with other new dog owners on the AKC's website (www.akc.org), Facebook (www.facebook.com/americankennelclub), and Twitter (@akcdoglovers). Happy training!

Sincerely,

Dennis B. Sprung
AKC President and CEO

Yes, There's a Right Way!

As the American Kennel Club slogan says, "We're more than champion dogs. We're the **dog's champion**." Promoting responsible dog ownership means helping dog lovers learn the right way to train and care for their dogs. To find the right way, we don't need to delve into stacks of training books or surf a million dog-related websites on the Internet. We can find all we need to know just by paying attention to the dog in our life, our cherished family companion. When a puppy yips happily, when an adult dog's eyes glisten with loyalty and trust, and when a senior dog's tail involuntarily wags when his neck is rubbed, it's about one thing. *Love*.

Undeniably, one of the most successful ways to train a dog is with love...and praise, patience, a little know-how, a lot of liver (a.k.a. rewards!), and more praise. In educating your puppy, you are teaching an intelligent, social animal how to please you and how to live among human society. The more a puppy understands what you expect from him, the happier and more secure he will feel and the more perfect will his behavior be!

The American Kennel Club's Train Your Puppy Right will give you the foundation you need to train your new canine companion to become a happy, self-assured member of your family. Beyond providing chapters on socialization, house-training, and basic obedience cues, this book introduces you to the exciting world of AKC events, such as Rally®, agility, and obedience trials. You will be amazed at the different ways you can become involved with your dog, such as taking an AKC S.T.A.R. Puppy® class or trying out the Coursing Ability Test. Maybe you'd like the experience of passing the Canine Good Citizen® test on your way to training for therapy work and receiving the AKC Therapy Dog title. As the "dog's champion," the American Kennel Club is dedicated to responsible dog ownership, and that includes providing you and your dog with educational programs, fun activities, and competitive events that will engage your family for years to come.

CHAPTER 1

A Puppy of Your Own

Congrats! You are now—or soon will be—the proud owner of the cutest puppy in the world! Let's face it, puppies are cute. They require a lot of love, patience, and understanding, just like all babies. Before you chose the breed of dog for you and found the perfect puppy, we hope you did your homework. If you're an "A" student, then you researched your breed on the AKC website (www.akc.org) and contacted someone from the national parent club to lead you to responsible, reliable breeders in your area. If you've found a good breeder and already picked out a puppy, you should be getting regular reports from the breeder about the first weeks of your puppy's life. Before the puppy is ready to come home with you, the breeder will give you information on his temperament, how he interacts with his siblings, and other tidbits about his personality. You may receive weekly photos of your puppy so you can see how quickly he's grown from a tiny teddy bear with closed eyes to an irresistible little pup who's bursting with energy and ready to meet you and see the wonderful world.

A good breeder will help you select the best puppy for you based on your lifestyle, the pups' personalities, and other important factors to ensure a suitable match.

While You Wait

Most breeders don't release puppies until they're eight to twelve weeks of age. The smaller the breed, the more likely the breeder will want to keep the puppies longer. Whether this is your first puppy or your dozenth, it's hard to bear the anticipation of a new puppy coming home for the first time. You can use this waiting time to do some research on your local doggy professionals. Look into veterinarians, groomers, and puppy classes in your area. Get to know your chosen breed better by picking up a book specifically about your breed if you haven't already done so. A good breed book can do wonders to acquaint you with the unique characteristics, needs, and personality of your breed. In addition, take this opportunity to look into the different types of sports and hobbies in which you and your dog can participate; some breeds are known to excel in certain areas. This is a great time to attend a dog show or a trial and talk with the participating dog owners. Contact an American Kennel Club-affiliated dog club to discover all the ways that you and your new puppy can get involved; you can find contact information for local clubs on the AKC's website.

Another way to kill some time (and money) before your puppy comes home is to go shopping! Wandering through a pet superstore is an adventure that every new puppy owner looks forward to. There are lots of great puppy items you'll want to stock up on ahead of time so that you have everything you need for your puppy's arrival. Collars, leashes, bowls, and bedding are just a few of the things you can begin looking for. The array of styles, colors, sizes, and innovations in pet products these days can make your puppy-supply shopping spree both exciting and a little overwhelming, not to mention expensive if you're not careful. However, having everything you need for the puppy's first week home allows you to enjoy your puppy's homecoming and not worry about emergency trips to the store for a bag of kibble or rolls of paper towels!

Shopping for Supplies

When you walk into a pet-supply superstore, you will be amazed by all of the products on display. These stores are virtual playgrounds of puppy toys and training equipment with supermarket-length aisles of dog food ranging from basic kibble to refrigerator cases of specialty foods. You'll find standard collars and leashes, but there are also harnesses, no-jump devices, halters, retractable leads, and a hundred other helpful tools—all to do something as simple as walk your dog! In truth, though, it's not the leash or collar you use as much as it is how you use them and how well you understand the basic principles of positive training, good socialization, and the importance of a loving, trusting relationship with your best friend.

Crate

More important than any dog bed or comfy pillow, a dog crate is one of the best things you'll ever purchase for your puppy. Your puppy's crate will quickly become his home within his home. It is a safe place where your puppy can relax, it helps keep him from getting into trouble around the house, and it is the most effective tool that you can use for house-training. Another important point that many people fail to consider is that if your dog is ever hospitalized or kenneled, he will be crated for his safety, and it will be much less stressful for him if he is already used to a crate. With comfortable bedding and a couple of favorite toys inside, your puppy's crate will become his very own bedroom.

Choose a crate for your puppy that will still be comfortable for him when he is a fully grown adult.

The two most popular types of crates are the wire crate and the plastic or fiberglass airline-type crate. The wire crate is collapsible and folds flat, making it easy to store or transport when empty, but can be heavier than the airline-style crate. Some people prefer the wire crate because it is more open, allowing the dog to see what is going on around him. A wire crate also often comes with an adjustable divider panel that enables you to make the puppy's area within the crate smaller while he is little and make it larger it as he grows.

With the best, soft-hearted intentions, many people put small puppies in jumbo crates, but a puppy's having too much room in a crate can lead to house-training issues. (It's very easy to sleep in the east wing and poop in the west!) If you prefer the wire crate, an adult-sized crate with a divider panel is a cost-effective choice that should last throughout your dog's lifetime.

If you purchased your dog from a breeder who is shipping the puppy to you, the puppy will most likely arrive in an appropriately sized airline crate. As long as the crate is not too big, you can use the same crate for house-training. An advantage of the airline-type crate is the fact that you can use it as your dog's special place and as a house-training tool, and you'll have it handy should the need arise for you to fly with your dog.

Many people like the airline-type crate because it offers a den-like area, is easy to clean, and doesn't make as much noise as a wire crate when the dog moves around in it. The ventilated door and panels on the sides of the crate keep the crate cool on warm days. The downside of the airline crate is that, should you decide to stop using it for a period of time, it is not as easy to store as a wire crate. It is recommended that you never get rid of your crate permanently, as you never know when you will need to use it again.

Bedding

During your puppy's first week at home with you, it's a great idea to give him a blanket or towel with the scent of his mother and littermates to sleep on (you can ask the breeder for

A bed gives your puppy a cozy place to curl up.

this when you pick up your puppy). This will ease his transition and help him adjust to his new home and crate. Once he settles in and starts sleeping through the night, you can observe the kind of sleeper he is and buy him some bedding based on the sleep position he likes best. Does he curl up in a ball or does he like to spread out?

There are many types of beds available. There are fleece mats in different sizes that are designed to fit inside crates perfectly. There are beds that are a bit thicker and resemble big flat pillows; these are great for dogs who like to sprawl out or lie on their sides. The bolster bed, or nest bed, is round like a donut and has an elevated roll around the edge for the dog to rest his head on; this is a good choice for the dog who prefers to curl up.

Grooming Tools

Even if you haven't purchased a puppy with a big, fluffy coat, such as a Poodle, Bichon Frise, or Samoyed, you will still need to brush your puppy. Dogs with the shortest coats still need to be groomed. There are many types of brushes on the market, and the right brush for your dog depends on his coat type. A pin brush has stiff wire bristles set in a rubber base and is used for single- or double-coated dogs with medium to long coats, such as Cavalier King Charles Spaniels and Australian Shepherds. The pin brush also works well on fine coats. A slicker brush has softer wire bristles and is great for removing the heavy undercoat on dogs such as Golden Retrievers and German Shepherd Dogs.

For a short-coated breed, such as a Bulldog or Doberman Pinscher, use a soft, short-bristled brush or "hound glove," which will be gentle on the coat and skin. Because dense, short coats are easy to comb through, it is not necessary to use a heavy brush or long-toothed comb designed for thicker coats; such a brush would be too harsh on the puppy's skin and coat.

Always keep a flea comb on hand, no matter what type of coat your dog has. A flea comb, which is a small metal comb with very close teeth, will help you find little black specks of "flea dirt," which is actually dried blood. Fleas move quickly and are difficult to see, so finding the dirt will help you determine their presence. Of course, at the first sign of fleas, you should address the problem.

A slicker brush penetrates thicker coats to get all the way down to the skin and remove dead coat.

Another important grooming tool is a sturdy pair of nail clippers. There are two types of nail clippers made for dogs: scissors-style and guillotine-style. Choose the type that you and your dog are comfortable with. It's also helpful to have silver nitrate or styptic powder on hand to stop the bleeding in case you clip a nail too short. Another option is a nail grinder, which some dogs prefer.

Bowls

Suppertime is every puppy's favorite time of day, followed by breakfast time, lunchtime, and afternoon treat time. You'll need something to serve your puppy's meals in, and the obvious answer is a bowl. There are dozens of dog-bowl options out there. The most sensible, if not the most attractive, are stainless-steel bowls—they will last almost forever and tend to be the easiest to clean, as they are nonporous and can be sanitized in the dishwasher. Plastic bowls, which come in various shapes, sizes, and depths, are usually less expensive but are not as durable, and they can harbor bacteria as the plastic gets scratched with use. Ceramic or earthenware bowls are very pretty and come in such an array of colors and patterns that you can actually coordinate your puppy's dishes with your kitchen decor if you like. However, young puppies tend to splash in their water and knock their bowls around, so save the breakable bowls until your pup matures a bit and isn't as active when eating and drinking.

Collars

Because his collar will mostly likely be your puppy's only item of clothing, let's select a collar with an eye on both function and fashion! It is important to have a collar ready for your puppy as soon as he comes home. Puppy collars are like baby clothes—tiny, adorable, and temporary. There are many collars out there, and it is important that your dog always wears at least a basic flat collar to hold his name tag. Your dog's everyday collar is different from the collar that he will wear for training purposes. The flat collar is the puppy's daywear and should stay on while the puppy is up and about, while the training collar will be removed after training sessions. For safety's sake, it's best to remove the puppy's collar whenever he's placed in his crate.

For your dog's everyday collar, there are two popular types: a nylon collar with a plastic clip or a nylon or leather collar with a metal buckle. You can adjust both types of collars as your puppy grows, but keep in mind that a metal buckle closure is more secure than a plastic clip closure.

Your puppy will also need a training collar; again, the only time that your puppy should wear a training collar is when you are training him and he is under your direct supervision. If you are not practicing obedience skills or teaching him how to walk on leash, be sure to remove the training collar.

The *fitted collar* (or *buckle collar*) sits high on a dog's neck, just below the ears. This is a great training collar for larger and older puppies, six months and up. If you feel behind the puppy's ears, there is a slight indentation where the collar should sit. It should fit snugly around his neck, so to buy the proper size, measure around your puppy's neck just behind the ears and add an inch. To adjust the collar to a proper fit, start with the dog facing you and place the collar around your dog's neck. Make sure that the snap is on your right and the end ring and the sliding ring are on your left. Attach the snap to the sliding ring, not the end ring, leaving about an inch of excess collar.

The *slip collar*, made of nylon, cotton rope, or leather, can be one of the safest training collars. When a slip collar is used properly, your puppy will not be stressed or uncomfortable, and he will not be able to escape as easily as with other collars. To ensure a proper fit, hold the collar with your left hand so that it hangs down vertically, and take the bottom ring in your right hand. Drop the rope into and through the bottom ring, still holding on to the bottom ring with your right hand. Bring your hands together and hold the rope with the fingers of your right hand; you will see that both rings are together. With both hands on the rope, turn it upside down and turn it around so that you are looking at the collar in the shape of the letter "P" (make sure it's not a backward "P"). Put the collar on your dog by putting his head through the top of the "P." This is easy to remember, as "P" stands for puppy!

The *martingale collar* has also been called the *Greyhound collar*. This collar tightens around the dog's neck when either you or the dog pulls on the leash, but it doesn't

A head halter, which sits on the dog's muzzle, can work well with some dogs.

break a dog's coat the way a nylon rope collar can. If you have a frisky dog, putting this collar on in the beginning will be difficult because you put it on over the dog's head and then adjust the size. Once the collar is on your dog, tighten it so that the two rings do not meet; if they do, the collar is too large. Attach the leash to the top ring, which allows the collar to tighten and release as you're training.

The *head halter* is more of a management tool than an optimum training tool. Sometimes inexperienced owners or trainers have a hard time fitting head halters correctly, and some dogs have difficulty getting used to the pressure on their muzzles, which can be even more stressful for them than a slip collar.

With a halter, start by making sure that you have the right size and type for your dog. To put it on, have the dog sit in front of you and, with your left hand, place the muzzle piece on first. Hold a treat in your right hand, in front of the muzzle, to encourage your dog to bring his head through the loop and take the treat. Be sure to give him lots of praise as he chews the treat. Next, put the collar part of the halter around the dog's neck and adjust the size, making sure that it is sitting high on the neck.

If your dog bucks like a bronco, stop and wait until he calms down. This is not the time to soothe him. If he drops to his belly and doesn't move, just be patient and don't pull on the leash. Be aware that a dog can slip out of a head halter, and you don't want a nervous, stressed dog running loose.

Leashes and Lines

Before you start training, get a thin, lightweight leash. Let your puppy get used to the leash by attaching it to his collar so he can drag it around the house while you're supervising. Also put the leash on for walks to his potty spot, which helps with the beginnings of leash training.

For small-breed puppies, such as Havanese and Chihuahuas, a basic 4-foot-long flat leash is ideal. For larger breeds, such as Golden Retrievers or Vizslas, trainers recommend a 5- or 6-foot-long leash for puppies. Leashes come in different widths, such as 1 inch, ¾ inch, and ½ inch. The ¾-inch width is best, as it is neither too wide nor too narrow for the average hand to grasp firmly and comfortably. Cotton and nylon are popular leash materials; however, leather leashes tend to be much more comfortable in the hand than cotton and nylon, and hemp leashes offer added strength and softness.

A *house line* is a leash that you want the puppy to wear around the house (under your supervision only). The best house line is a lightweight round nylon lead, about 3 to 4 feet long, no matter your puppy's breed or size. A round leash will not wrap around the legs of furniture and get stuck the way a flat leash can.

The purpose of the house line is to allow you to stop the puppy from doing something you don't want him to do, such as taking off with your favorite shoes or grabbing the end of the toilet paper roll and dragging the paper across the house. You can simply grab the

For a strong large-breed puppy, purchase a thick, sturdy leash.

leash, bring the puppy toward you, ask for the item by saying "Give," and then gently remove the item from his mouth. When he releases the item, tell him "Good dog!"

Another benefit of the house line is that if you see the puppy starting to relieve himself in the house, you can easily interrupt his accident by grabbing the line and making a lot of noise as you rush him out the door to finish up. It is more difficult for your puppy to run away from you if he is dragging the line behind him, making it easier for you to grab hold of the line. The ability to catch your puppy in the act and correct him will create consistency in your training.

Identification

Some things never go out of style, and dog tags top this list. Today's ID tags go way beyond engraved stainless-steel plates. There's everything from bronze- or gold-plated tags and slide-on tags to designer bone-shaped tags and electronic devices. Whatever style you decide upon, make sure it's firmly attached to your dog's everyday collar. You can purchase the tag well in advance of your puppy's arrival home. For security reasons and to prevent pet theft, don't put your dog's name on the tag. It is also recommended that you list just your cell phone number so that someone who finds your dog can reach you even if you are away from home.

As handy as the ID tag is, it's not a permanent way to identify your dog. Take advantage of modern technology and have your puppy microchipped. If his collar or tag comes off, the microchip is your saving grace. A microchip is the size of a grain of rice and inserted under the puppy's skin between the shoulder blades. The radio-activated chip can be scanned by animal shelters, police departments, and veterinarians' offices should your dog get lost and end up in one of these places. A unique number registered to you, along with the pet-recovery service's information, is revealed once the chip is scanned. Whoever has your dog calls the pet-recovery service, who then contacts you to let you know that your dog has been found. You must register your microchip with the pet-recovery service and be sure to always maintain a copy of the registration paperwork so you will know how to contact the company and update your information when needed.

The American Kennel Club Companion Animal Recovery (AKC CAR) service offers a lifetime of around-the-clock protection in the event that your dog gets lost or stolen. The AKC CAR service will register any microchip, regardless of manufacturer, so that all of your pets can be registered together, which enables you to update your contact information seamlessly. For more information about the AKC CAR's services and getting your pet microchipped, visit www.akccar.org.

Do not underestimate the importance of identification throughout your dog's life. Do not think that your puppy will grow up to become "street smart"—he won't ever know to stay out of roads and away from traffic. Once they are lost, most dogs don't find their way home on their own, so it is important to never allow your puppy or adult dog to roam freely through your neighborhood or run around in an unfenced yard. Not only can your dog become lost, he could also be stolen.

Even if identified by another method, your puppy should have an ID tag securely attached to his everyday collar.

A durable chew bone exercises your puppy's jaws and gives him relief from teething pain.

Toys

These days it seems that FAO Schwartz or the elves from up North are stocking the toy aisles at pet-supply superstores! Every toy you can imagine, far beyond your pup's wildest daydreams, can be found at your local pet-supply store. While they haven't commercially released a robot that will throw the tennis ball for you, they've pretty much come up with everything else. Take some time to explore the future contents of your puppy's toy box. Your puppy can enjoy an array of interactive toys, such as those that dispense treats as dogs play with them; retrieving toys, such as flying discs and erratically bouncing balls; chew toys, such as rubber puppy "binkies" and teething rings, nylon and rawhide bones, and twisted ropes; and fun-to-love toys, such as plush animals, squeaky balls, and vinyl novelties. And, of course, if the variety is just too overwhelming for you, there's always a tennis ball and an empty plastic milk jug!

TASTY TOYS

Peanut butter always makes play more fun! And so does liver! Treat-release toys are great fun and provide dogs with necessary mental exercise. A basic type of treat-release toy has small holes in it that allow treats to spill out randomly as the dog rolls it around; more complex types require the dog to press a lever or move some parts around before the food will come out. You can fill these toys with small dog treats or pieces of your dog's dry food—and watch your dog do the rest.

Monitor the condition of any soft or plush toys, as an enthusiastic chewer can destroy them in short order.

CHAPTER 2

A Puppy in Your Home

It's Day One for your puppy! The video camera is charged, the pantry is stocked with the best puppy food and training treats, and the whole family is cast in the puppy's homecoming parade. Before you cue the trombones to strike up the band, take a giant step backward and think "less is more." Your puppy's first day home is more exciting for you than for your puppy—for him, this day can be overwhelming, upsetting, and traumatic.

Until the drive (or possibly flight!) to your home, your puppy spent all of his time learning proper pack behavior from his dam and littermates and getting basic socialization from the breeder and his or her family or assistants. Suddenly, the puppy is removed from his mother and siblings and sent to a foreign land. Well, to a puppy, your home, with new people (and maybe young people), strange sounds and smells, and maybe a cat or two, must seem like a foreign land. Introducing him to a new place, where his pack is now a bunch of strange humans, requires him to learn a completely

With all of the new sights, sounds, smells—and of course, people—puppy's first day home can be exhausting!

new way of life without the comfort and support of his mother and siblings. The puppy is now the center of attention, and he is faced with the daunting task of learning how to behave in this unfamiliar human world.

Don't overdo it or overwhelm him, and make sure everyone in your home gets that memo. Have the whole family agree on the house rules and be consistent about how they are to enforce these rules. Everyone should handle the puppy gently and carefully. Save the "pass the puppy" game for next week, along with his introduction to every neighbor, neighbor's dog, and delivery person.

If yours is a home with children, there's the potential for confusion and inconsistency when training the puppy. For example, Dad may enjoy roughhousing with the puppy and allowing the pup to chew on his hands and arms, but little Annie just wants the puppy to allow her to pet him calmly. The more inconsistency in the household rules, the more likely the dog will misbehave because he doesn't understand what is expected of him.

It is important that the children in the household are first taught how to interact properly with the puppy. They should not yank on the puppy's tail, spank him, or throw their toy trucks at him. Children also have to remember that the puppy will need to sleep a lot and should not be bothered when sleeping or eating. His crate needs to be respected, and he must be allowed to sleep in peace. If you're both a parent and a new puppy owner, you owe it to the new puppy to make sure that your children adhere to the rules and do not jeopardize the puppy's training, confidence, or safety. Explain all of these things carefully to your children before the puppy comes home and be prepared to remind them regularly once the puppy is home with you.

To gain the full benefits of proper house-training, everyone must know the puppy's potty schedule. For example, first thing in the morning, no one should release the puppy from his crate for playtime before he has been taken outside to relieve himself. If you have young children who have a hard time following these rules, get a lock for the crate door. If you have children who are too young to walk the dog by themselves, they can still participate in the puppy's house-training if accompanied by an adult who will hold the leash when outside for the dog's safety.

Puppy-Proofing

It is important to puppy-proof the house before bringing the puppy home. Think of it as though you were bringing a baby home—a baby who is going to crawl over, chew on, bite, and pull anything that he or she sees. The best way to puppy-proof your home is to get on your hands and knees and crawl around to see your house from your puppy's perspective to see what will be in his line of sight.

The first things to look for are loose electrical cords and cables, floor lamps that could be easily knocked over, shoes, clothing, children's toys, and anything else that the puppy could ingest or break. Keep all plants completely out of your puppy's reach, meaning up off the floor with no leaves or branches hanging where puppy can grab them. A knocked-over plant will be messy at the very least, but it can also injure your puppy or cause serious illness or even death if it is one of the many common plants that are toxic to dogs. Some poisonous plants include lily of the valley, hibiscus, hydrangea, oleander, azalea, rhododendron, and kalanchoe.

Anything that hangs down will tease a young puppy—think tablecloths, curtains, fabrics with fringes, and toilet paper hanging from the roll. Also look out for items on tabletops that the puppy can reach with his mouth or paws if he gets up on his hindquarters. You will be surprised

A curious puppy could become injured or ill from exploring certain common plants.

by how determined a puppy can be when he wants something. Watch out for books or trinkets on low shelves, not only those at mouth level but also those at tail level. A frisky moving tail can sweep heavy objects off a table or bookshelf.

Puppies have been known to open cabinets, refrigerators, and pantry doors in the most shocking ways. Some dogs of larger breeds have been known to wrap their mouths around doorknobs to open them. It is recommended that you get childproof locks, which are very easy to install. You can get them at hardware stores or anywhere that sells baby supplies. You don't want your puppy stealing tomorrow's dinner, and you especially don't want your puppy to get into any hazardous materials that you may have under the kitchen sink or in your medicine cabinet.

Here are a few other things to watch out for when puppy-proofing your home:

Children's toys: Many children's toys come with warnings stating that they contain small parts, could be choking hazards, or are appropriate for children only of a certain age. These warnings also apply to puppies, who will put parts in their mouths and chew and/or swallow small pieces. Your child may end up missing important pieces to a favorite game or a button from a beloved doll's dress; more importantly, the puppy could choke or end up with a dangerous blockage that requires very expensive surgery. A good rule of thumb to follow is if a child's toy is smaller than the puppy, the toy should be put away when not in use in a place where the puppy cannot get to it.

Furniture: Wood and leather are attractive to a chewing puppy, so if you have wooden or leather furniture, you may want to use a bitter-tasting chew-deterrent product on it. First, test a small patch in a hidden area to be sure that the product won't damage your furniture. Once you have decided that it is safe to put on the furniture, apply the product to your puppy's favorite chew spot—for example, the leg of a chair—and then bring him over to the furniture. Encourage the puppy to lick the chair leg with the product freshly applied; the unpleasant taste will teach your puppy very quickly to avoid the furniture.

Some people opt to cover all of their furniture with sheets until the puppy grows up and out of the chewing stage. Regardless of what precautions you take with your furniture, it is important that your puppy has a variety of sturdy chew toys, as this will decrease his likelihood of chewing on anything inappropriate.

The yard: Don't forget to puppy-proof your yard; this is just as important

ELECTRICAL DANGERS

Phone wires and electrical cords are a chewing puppy's dream, but these of course are big no-nos. Not only can your puppy potentially electrocute himself in the worst case, but you could end up with an antique lamp that needs rewiring or is pulled down and broken into pieces. Tie up any loose cords that you find; you can also place the cords inside PVC piping to inhibit chewing.

A garden hose or a giant chew toy? Your new puppy won't make the distinction.

as the inside of the house. While it is never suggested that you leave your puppy alone outside for any reason, you still need to puppy-proof the yard. There are many dangers outdoors, and puppies can get into the most surprising things right in front of you.

Start by taking a "puppy's-eye-view" look at your yard. It is important to store hoses, ladders, bags of potting soil, lawn-care chemicals, and gardening tools in safe areas, just as you would inside the house. As previously mentioned, certain plants are very poisonous to dogs. If you don't know what types of plants and bushes you have in your yard, now's the time to find out. Talk to someone at your local garden center about dog-safe replacements for any toxic plants that you find.

There are many pet-safe ways to care for your lawn; look for pet-friendly lawn and garden products online or at your local garden center. The safest fertilizer for your lawn, though, is compost, which is easily produced using leaves and your leftover vegetables and fruits. In traditional fertilizers, two of the most toxic ingredients are metaldehyde and disulfoton. It is important that you examine the ingredients of any garden product and research before using it so that you don't put anything in your garden or on your lawn that could cause your dog harm if he ingests it or gets it on his skin.

If you have a swimming pool, it is important to teach your puppy to swim—even though you should never leave him unattended in the pool area. In any case, it is a good idea to put up a fence around the pool, as even the best canine swimmers have been known to fall into family pools and drown.

There are also hazards in the garage and shed. Antifreeze can taste quite good to a dog but can be fatal if ingested. Paints, paint thinners, solvents, and insecticides are other items that need to be locked up so that your puppy cannot get to them.

Chocolate and other food: Chocolate contains theobromine, which your dog's liver cannot metabolize; it will quickly kill your dog. If you think that your dog has eaten some chocolate, call your veterinarian right away to determine the course of action to take. Depending on how much chocolate the dog ingested (if known) and how much time has elapsed, you may be told to bring your dog in to see the vet or you may be instructed on how to induce vomiting at home.

Other foods that can be toxic to your dog include apples, apricots, cherries, peaches, plums, onions, garlic, coffee grounds, macadamia nuts, grapes, and raisins.

The First Day and Night

As everyone knows, dogs sniff first and ask questions later. Playing to your puppy's super-keen nose, you can begin getting acquainted with your pup before he comes home by sharing something fresh out of your hamper. If possible, bring one of your unwashed shirts to the breeder three to five days before you pick your puppy up. Ask the breeder to let the puppy sleep with the shirt so that he becomes familiar with your scent before he comes home with you. Also ask the breeder if you can take home a toy and blanket with the scent of his mother and littermates on them. Place these items in the puppy's crate so that he is comforted by the familiar scent when he first comes home with you.

When the big day arrives, if you are driving to get your puppy, make sure that you have his crate in the car; it is too dangerous to travel with your puppy loose in the car. Put the bedding with the scent of his littermates, along with your unwashed shirt, in the crate for the ride home. You will also want to bring his leash and collar. Keep them on him while he is in the crate so if he should escape the crate for any reason, you will be able to easily and safely catch him. Stock the car with paper towels and plastic bags in case of a potty accident.

That being said, it is safest for you to keep the puppy in his crate until you return home rather than stopping on the side of the road to let him go potty. Do your best to make sure that he relieves himself before you leave the breeder. Your puppy is already in a strange situation, and you don't want him to become startled by something, such as the sound of truck backfiring, and slip free from

Give your resident dog a chance to get used to the newcomer.

his collar and run onto the highway or elsewhere into danger. It is best to wait until you get home to let the puppy have a bathroom break.

If your new puppy is an "only child," you can bring him straight home. If you have another dog, plan to meet a friend or family member with your resident dog at a nearby park or other dog-friendly location—somewhere other than your home so that the dog and puppy can meet in a neutral environment. Let them sniff each other and play a bit before bringing them back to the house together.

Once home, walk your puppy around the yard and take him wherever it is that you will want him to go to the bathroom. Give him a few minutes to walk around and sniff the area while on leash. If he goes to the bathroom, praise him and bring him inside. Allow him to sniff and run around the house under supervision for a few minutes; keep the leash on him so that, if needed, you'll be able to get him outside again quickly or stop him from doing something that you don't want him to do. After a short session of exploring, place your puppy in his crate for a good nap. He has had a tiring day so far. After his nap, you can begin your house-training program.

When it's time for bed, put the puppy's crate for the first night in your bedroom so that your puppy feels that he is part of the pack. You can wrap a ticking clock in some blankets for the first night—the sound will soothe him, but keep the clock outside the crate. Be sure to put the blanket with his littermates' and mother's scent in the crate with him. You can also place another towel or blanket in the dryer a few minutes before you put him into bed so that he sleeps with a nice, warm blanket.

Grooming

It's a good thing that puppy coats don't need to be brushed as often as adult coats. Puppies of high-maintenance breeds, such as Poodles, Pomeranians, and West Highland White Terriers, don't require much grooming until their coats begin to grow...and grow and grow. Owners can take advantage of the easy-care puppy coat to slowly get their pups accustomed to the grooming routine. Your professional groomer will thank you when your adolescent Poodle, Pom, or Westie is a polite and patient client who's a pleasure to groom.

With all dogs, regardless of coat type or length, brushing keeps the skin healthy and the coat clean and tangle-free; it also exfoliates dead skin and keeps the healthy oils circulating through the coat. During your regular brushing sessions, you'll be able to find any parasites before they become a problem and check for any scratches, cuts, or other abnormalities.

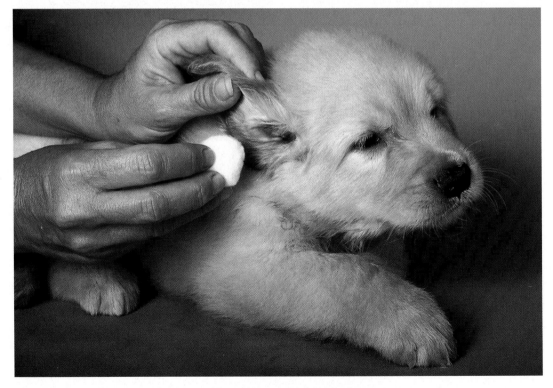

All breeds benefit from having their ears checked regularly and cleaned as needed.

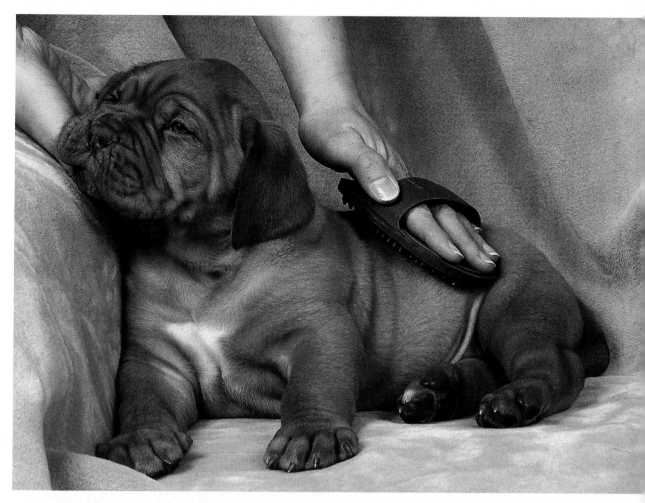

A grooming tool with rubber knobs helps keep a short coat clean and shiny.

Obviously, different breeds have different grooming needs. For example, a Standard Poodle needs to be groomed daily, and a Whippet can be groomed weekly. There are different brushes for different coat types, and it is important that you seek the help of a professional when dealing with heavily coated breeds, such as the Poodle, Puli, or Pekingnese, that require more maintenance.

All dogs need to be bathed, but most don't need frequent baths. Bathing any dog too often could dry out his skin. You want your dog to maintain the natural oils in his skin, and too-frequent bathing can create skin problems that become a vicious cycle to correct. The general rule of shampoo is: the more coat your dog has, the more often he'll need a bath. Most show dogs are bathed before each show, especially the ones with the big coats. If your puppy rolls in something too nasty for words, decides to paddle through a mud puddle, or starts to look a little dingy, you'll need to get out the shampoo. In other words, you'll know when it's time for a bath!

Most dogs don't appreciate the joys of a good mani/pedi, but, even so, nail trimming is a vital part of every dog's grooming routine. If a dog's nails are too long, they can create problems when he walks. Buy a quality nail clipper or grinder and start trimming your puppy's nails when he is young so that he gets used to it. You can start by gently massaging your puppy's feet so that he becomes comfortable with having his feet handled.

The best way to start trimming a puppy's nails is to place him in your lap as if you were cuddling with him. Keep treats nearby but out of the puppy's reach so that he can't steal them from you without earning them.

1. Hold one of the puppy's paws and touch the paw with the nail clipper.
2. Give the puppy a small treat.
3. Repeat with each foot.
4. Go back to the first foot and clip one nail at a time, giving a small treat after each nail.

If your puppy is still calm after you've clipped each nail on the first foot, move on to the next foot. Even if you can finish only one foot in a session, it's still a terrific start.

Make sure that you initially simply graze the tip of the nail so that your puppy gets used to the sensation. You don't want to take off too much, as you could clip the nail too short, and all that you're really aiming for at this point is to get your puppy used to the feeling of the clipper on his nails.

The *quick* is a vein that runs through the center of each nail. On white nails, you can detect the quick by looking for where the nail turns pink. On black nails, you can find

Hold your pup in your lap as you work on his nails so that you can comfort him as you clip.

the quick by looking under the nail to see where it becomes thicker. Position your clipper close to the end of the nail, away from the quick, so that you do not nip the quick and make the nail bleed.

Check your puppy's nails regularly, about once a week. How often you need to trim them depends on if he plays mostly indoors or on grass or if he often walks on pavement. If your dog is usually on concrete, his nails are constantly being ground down as he walks, so you likely won't need to clip them as often.

Let's not forget your dog's pearly whites. Clean teeth and fresh breath are virtues in human society, so investing some time in your dog's dental care will make you smile, too. Too many owners don't realize the importance of good dental hygiene for their dogs. It's not just about clean breath—though that's nice—it's about

Don't neglect your puppy's teeth! Accustom him to having his mouth handled early on.

good health. Every puppy needs dental care at home from an early age. Periodontal diseases such as gingivitis can be caused by poor oral hygiene. When you first get your puppy, start familiarizing him with having his teeth cleaned every day to keep plaque and tartar to a minimum. Your veterinarian should check your dog's teeth and gums at every checkup.

The best way to brush your puppy's teeth is with a small rubber fingertip brush, which can be found at any pet-supply store. Be sure to use toothpaste made for dogs, as human toothpaste can be toxic to dogs. To begin:

1. Hold your puppy gently in your lap.
2. Take a treat in one hand and rub the puppy's gums with a finger on your other hand.
3. Give your puppy the treat.
4. Repeat the process, keeping your finger in his mouth a little longer each time so that he gets used to having your hands in his mouth.
5. Introduce the fingertip toothbrush, at first for just short periods of time and gradually building up to longer brushing sessions.
6. When your puppy tolerates having the toothbrush in his mouth for longer periods of time, add some toothpaste.
7. Work up to brushing all of his teeth and his gums.

Visiting the Vet and Vaccinations

While you can be your puppy's dentist at home, you can't be his doctor, so you need to find a good veterinarian in your area. With any luck, you have dog-owning friends who can make recommendations. You can also use the AKC's website (www.akc.org) to find a veterinarian, though the club is not affiliated with and does not endorse any vet. Follow your gut instinct— if you meet the vet and get a good feeling about him or her, you're probably in good hands.

The first part of your trip to the vet is making sure that your new puppy is traveling safely in your car. Transporting your puppy in his crate is the best idea; however, if this is not possible, invest in a seat-belt harness for dogs, which can be found at pet-supply stores.

If using a seat belt with your puppy, the right side of the back seat is the safest place to put him. This way, you can see him easily through the rearview mirror or by glancing over your right shoulder while driving. If he is behind you, he might paw at you while you are driving. The front seat is not safe for various reasons: one is that he may preoccupy himself with trying to climb into your lap while you are driving, and another is that if you get into an accident and the airbag goes off, it could seriously injure or possibly kill your puppy. Practice putting the seat belt on the puppy before your trip and adjust it for a proper fit; a puppy can wiggle his way out of an incorrectly fitted seat belt, which defeats the purpose of having one.

It is a good idea to get your new puppy to the veterinarian within two or three days of picking him up from the breeder. You want to make sure that the puppy receives a clean bill of health. There are a few things you can do at home to prepare puppy for his veterinary visit and make it as pleasant as possible for him:

- Try to make a practice trip to the vet's office before puppy's first appointment. It is a good idea to allow the pup to meet and receive treats from the office staff so that his first experience at the vet's office is positive instead of filled with shots.

Choose a vet with whom both you and your puppy are comfortable.

- Handle your puppy all over his body so that he won't be startled by the vet's examination. Touch his teeth, massage each of the pads of his feet, gently turn him over and pet his belly, and even touch his rear end and gently move his tail around (the vet or vet tech may do this to take his temperature). As you are handling him, give him small food tidbits so that it is a very positive, enjoyable experience for him.
- Do not feed your pup a meal within three hours of the trip to decrease his chances of getting sick in the car.

At the first visit, your vet will do a full examination of your puppy, which will include listening to his heart, taking his temperature, and weighing him. When you make your appointment, the office staff will most likely ask you to bring in a stool sample. You can either use stool from the day of his appointment or, if necessary, take one from the day before, place it in a small plastic bag, and refrigerate it until you go to your appointment.

There are two commands—*stand* and *stay*—that you will find helpful for veterinary visits. Your puppy's knowledge of these commands will make the examination much easier for the veterinarian and less stressful for your pup, and it will help your visit go much more smoothly and swiftly in general.

Your puppy may be due for vaccinations at his first appointment; if not, you and the vet will discuss the timing of future vaccinations. The *core* vaccines recommended

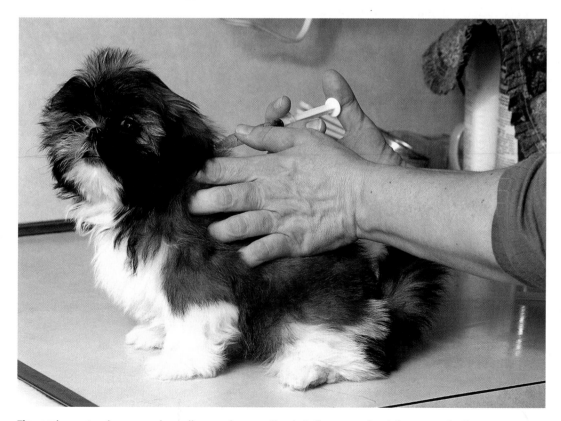

The vaccine protocol may vary depending on where you live, but all pups need certain core vaccinations.

by the American Veterinary Medical Association for all puppies by sixteen weeks of age are distemper, hepatitis, and parvovirus. By the time your puppy comes home with you, he should have received his first round of distemper, hepatitis, and parvovirus vaccines, which may have been combined into one shot, called DHPP (distemper, hepatitis [adenovirus type 2], parvovirus, and parainfluenza). The breeder should send you home with your puppy's health records, which will document which vaccines have been given and when. The DHPP is administered again between ten and twelve weeks of age and again between fourteen and sixteen weeks of age. The rabies vaccine is mandated by law and is given around sixteen weeks of age or older; check your local regulations.

Certain optional, or *noncore*, vaccines may be important for your dog depending on where you live and where he will be spending time. For example, the vet may suggest the *Bordetella* (kennel cough) vaccine if your puppy will be around groups of puppies, such as in training classes or at doggy day care. Vaccines to protect your puppy from leptospirosis, coronavirus, Lyme disease, and *Giardia* are others that the vet may discuss with you.

Don't forget to talk to your vet at your first visit about parasite-prevention options. There are topical products that are applied between the dog's shoulder blades monthly to protect against fleas and ticks, and there are monthly heartworm preventatives that are given orally. Often, the veterinarian will recommend a combination of the two, as the oral medication will also kill other types of worms that your puppy can contract.

The topic of spaying and neutering will likely come up at your first veterinary visit as well. *Spaying* is a surgical procedure in which a female dog is put under general anesthesia, and her ovaries, uterus, and fallopian tubes are removed. Recovery takes a few days, and the vet will ask you to bring your puppy back about ten days after the surgery for suture removal. *Neutering* is a procedure in which a male dog's testicles are removed.

Many vets recommend that you have your dog spayed or neutered between five and eight months of age. There are tremendous advantages to having your female spayed prior to her first heat cycle; for example, her chances of developing mammary-gland

GOOD FOOD, HEALTHY PUPPY

It is important to consult your puppy's breeder and your veterinarian before changing your puppy's food. Initially, it is best to continue feeding your puppy the same food that the breeder was feeding him; don't change too much too soon. If you decide to make a switch, do it over a few days to avoid stomach upset. Start by feeding 75 percent old food and 25 percent new food on the first day, then 50 percent old food and 50 percent new food for the next two days, then 25 percent old food and 75 percent new food for a day before switching over to just the new food.

cancer will be less than 1 percent. The benefits of neutering male dogs are also numerous—neutering helps eliminate prostate problems, reduce aggression, and decrease the dog's tendency to engage in behaviors such as humping, wandering, and urine marking.

Keeping Your Puppy Safe

Puppies are like small children who have not yet figured out how to keep themselves safe and do not understand the potential dangers that exist around them; thus, it our responsibility to keep our puppies safe at all times and to be diligent and careful in all situations with them.

Introducing the Car

The car ride home from the breeder was probably your puppy's first time in the family car. The breeder may have taken him for short rides for socialization or to the vet, but you'll need to do a little work to accustom him to the car after he comes home with you. Start by taking the puppy for short car trips around town, such as dropping the kids off at school or filling up at the gas station. Never take him anywhere that will require you to leave him alone in the car; that is a big no-no for all dogs of any age.

To accustom your puppy to riding in the car, start off with trips no more than fifteen minutes long. Try to initially travel on straight, less-traveled roads rather than very curvy, congested roads. Make sure that it is nice and cool in the car for the puppy, and avoid driving too fast or making a lot of sudden stops. Do not feed your puppy right before the car ride; in fact, try to wait about four hours after mealtime to take your puppy in the car to avoid carsickness.

Once your puppy has gotten used to short rides, slowly build up to rides of about thirty minutes in length. Once your puppy does well with these longer rides, build up to forty-five minutes and then to an hour.

The crate protects your dog during travel and also can make him feel more at ease in the car.

When out with your puppy, take the opportunity to teach him how to behave in all situations.

Remember, the safest place for your puppy in the car is in a crate; you can either put him in his own crate or purchase a separate travel crate. The crate protects your puppy from getting hurt should you get into an accident, and it also stops your puppy from climbing around the car or into your lap while you are driving, which is dangerous for all concerned. You may think that you can handle driving with a small dog on your lap or even on a passenger's lap, but dogs have minds of their own—you never know what they are going to do. Your dog could jump down near your feet and get in the way of the pedals. If someone else hits you and your airbag goes off while your dog is in your lap, it will kill him instantly. Place your dog's crate in the backseat. If your car won't accommodate a crate, get your dog a safety harness that attaches to a seat belt.

It is very important to lock your windows if your car has power windows and your dog is not confined to a crate. Your puppy can easily paw at the window button to roll it down and stick his head out, only to push the button again and close the window on himself. That is a very dangerous situation for the puppy and for the driver. It is not a good idea to let your dog stick his head out of the window in any case, as dirt or debris can easily fly into his eyes.

Door Safety

It is important that your puppy knows how to go through doors safely. Teach him to always sit and stay before he exits or enters through a door.

It's also helpful to teach your dog how to go through a revolving door. The best way to go through a revolving door is one step at a time with your dog on your right-hand side, where there is more room, instead of in the traditional *heel* position on your left-hand side. Go very slowly, taking a step and letting your dog come forward with you. The next step is to push the door a little farther forward, take another step, and let your dog step forward with you. Once you practice this a few times slowly, your dog will be able to go through a revolving door easily. Be careful of automatic revolving doors, as your dog may not move quickly enough and can get hurt.

Stair Safety

Whether or not you have stairs in your home or live in an apartment building with stairs, it is important that you teach your puppy how to go up and down stairs, as you never know when you will come across them or need to use them in a hurry.

Start by bringing your puppy to the bottom of the stairs and move his feet for him, forequarters followed by hindquarters, up one stair at a time. You may have to do this for the entire flight of stairs, up and back down, but make sure that you have your puppy on leash and don't let him chicken out. Just go up and down a flight of stairs once a day, and in a few days' time he will be navigating the stairs with no problem.

Elevator Safety

Apartment dwellers have to be very careful when getting onto an elevator with a puppy. If your dog runs ahead or lags behind on his leash, the door can close on the leash, leaving you in a dangerous situation with the leash handle on one side and your dog on the other side. Always make sure that your dog's whole body (including his tail!) is inside the elevator; he needs to walk close to your side. When you get to the elevator, follow these steps:

1. Place your dog in a *sit/stay* while you're waiting.
2. When the door opens, stick your arm out across the doorway to stop the doors from closing, and walk in together.
3. Keep your arm in the doorway until you are both fully inside, then place your dog in a *sit/stay*.
4. Repeat these steps when you are exiting the elevator.

CHAPTER 3

The Social Puppy

Dog books are always talking about "proper socialization," which is a very formal way of saying "get out there and mix it up!" Your puppy needs to meet lots of new people and other dogs so that he can learn how to interact with others. On his daily walk, he should meet your neighbors and the mail carrier. At the shopping plaza, he can meet strangers and their (hopefully well-behaved) children. At the park, he can meet other dogs and find out how to communicate with members of his own species that he doesn't know. He will see, hear, and smell new things everywhere he goes!

It sounds easy and fun, and it is, but it's also more important than you realize. You are ensuring that your puppy will grow up into a well-balanced adult dog who is comfortable around all kinds of people and other dogs as well as in various situations. Proper socialization, or lack thereof, during the puppy's first weeks at home will affect the dog throughout his lifetime. Psychology professors J. Paul Scott and John Fuller, in their seminal work

During their early weeks with their littermates, puppies begin developing their social skills.

Genetics and Social Behavior of the Dog, state that the most important time for a puppy's socialization is between three and twelve weeks of age. That doesn't give new owners much time at all to hesitate, as most puppies come home at around eight weeks of age. Proper socialization builds a dog's trust and helps teach him how to deal with stressful circumstances. It helps develop a bright, adaptable, and healthy mind that will make training more fun and effective for your puppy.

Socializing Your Puppy

There are many great ways to socialize your new puppy. It doesn't take a lot of planning, but it does require you to leave the house. You don't have to be too regimented; some spontaneity adds variety to the mix. Continually introducing your puppy to different scenarios and stimuli helps him develop confidence in new situations and helps desensitize him to potentially frightening events. Make an effort to take your puppy out every day, going to new places and meeting new people. One socialization date a week is not enough. Your puppy needs to be stimulated and exposed to new environments on an ongoing basis. The more often you take your puppy out, the better he will fare in unfamiliar circumstances.

Puppy Party

How about planning a "puppy party" or "doggy mixer"? Invite your friends, along with their well-behaved children and dogs, to meet and play with your new puppy. You can do this with your young pup after he's had a few days to settle in, as long as you make certain that all of the other dogs are current on their vaccinations and play nicely with small puppies.

Each human guest takes some time to pet the puppy and give him some affection.

No puppy party is complete without a good game of "pass the puppy," which is more of a hand-off than a pass. All it takes is for everyone to sit in a circle and take turns holding, petting, and talking to the puppy. As each person holds the puppy, he or she must do the following:

- Make funny sounds, such as whistles and siren-like howls, to get the puppy used to different and startling noises. Someone who is not sitting in the circle can incorporate loud sounds by dropping a pot on the floor, for example.
- Speak in different voices—loud, soft, booming, high-pitched, and so on—to accustom the puppy to different people.
- Hold the puppy; rub his belly, his ears, and his tail, and give him a big hug. This will get him used to being touched. Some puppies are very touch-sensitive, which can lead to aggression problems in the future, so the sooner you desensitize the puppy to touch, the better. He needs to tolerate being handled by the veterinarian, having his ears and teeth cleaned,

Adults must instruct their children and any young visitors how to properly and gently handle the puppy.

and having his nails clipped. Hugging the puppy will accustom him to clumsy handling, such as that of a child.

Let the other dogs do their own thing—they can wander around, approach the puppy, and play calmly. Don't let them be too rowdy in play, and any aggression must not be tolerated. They should all have leashes attached to their collars so they can be grabbed and pulled away quickly if needed.

When inviting canine guests to your puppy party, do not include adult dogs whose size or energy level could be intimidating to your new puppy. For example, you do not want an active adult Labrador Retriever with your tiny Maltese puppy. The Labrador will not know his own strength and could easily injure, albeit unintentionally, such a small, young dog.

Dog Parks

Dog parks are great places to socialize your puppy once you get clearance from your veterinarian that your puppy has received sufficient vaccinations and it's safe for him to visit a dog park. It is important to remember that your young puppy, even if he is a large-breed puppy, is small and shouldn't be around large adult dogs right away. Visit a dog park that has a small-dog area so your puppy can play with dogs his size.

The first few times, visit the dog park when it is a bit quieter. On weekdays, dog parks are usually very busy in the early morning hours and after work, so it is best to go later in the morning or in the early afternoon when it's less crowded and your puppy won't be overwhelmed. Make sure that the temperature outside is comfortable for your puppy, and bring along some fresh, cool water for him.

All puppies have different reactions to dog parks. Some sit and observe as they get a feel for the environment. Some walk around slowly and sniff, while others embrace the opportunity to run free. Let your puppy explore the dog park however he wants. If he is not interested in meeting other dogs immediately, there is nothing wrong with that; not all dogs in the park play with each other. Let your puppy become acclimated in his own way.

If your puppy takes off and runs around with abandon, wait until he settles down before calling him to you. If you start calling your puppy and he does not respond, he will learn that he does not have to listen to what you say, so it is very important that you don't issue any cues that you are unable to enforce.

Many puppies enjoy the sights, smells, sounds, and off-leash time provided by the dog park.

DOG-PARK ETIQUETTE

Dog parks can be great places not only for socializing your puppy but also for you to enjoy meeting other dog owners. If you have a very sensitive puppy, visit the dog park at a time when you know that there will be very few dogs there, such as midmorning or early afternoon. Alternatively, you can walk your puppy around the park a few times before going into the fenced dog area. Three to five visits like this should pique your puppy's curiosity and accustom him to the sights, sounds, and smells of the dog park before he actually goes inside and is greeted by a bunch of unfamiliar dogs who will want to sniff him all over. All young puppies should go into the small-dog run, if there is one.

Bring water and clean-up bags with you, but do not bring treats or any of your puppy's toys, because those items give him something to guard and could start a fight. The only collar that your puppy should wear is a flat buckle collar with his ID tag attached. You do not want your puppy to wear any type of collar that is designed to tighten and loosen.

For your puppy's safety, pay attention to him and the other dogs. Talking on the phone, listening to music, or texting are not good ideas. It takes only a split second for something to happen and a fight to break out. Do not let your puppy bother other dogs, and if you notice dogs who are not getting along with each other, bring it to the attention of the other owners. It is our responsibility to protect our own dogs as well as to protect other dogs from troublemakers. If your puppy is sexually mature or close to it and has not been neutered or spayed yet, be very careful about your puppy's interactions with other dogs.

When entering and exiting the dog park, close each gate behind you and make sure that it is securely latched. Do not open the second gate without making sure that the first gate is closed properly, and pay attention to any dogs who may be trying to sneak in and out.

If you follow these no-nonsense rules, you and your pup will have an enjoyable time at the dog park.

Walks around town offer wonderful socialization opportunities and time to practice good manners in public.

Out and About

During the busy days of puppyhood, caffeine can't be a bad thing—for you (not the puppy!). An espresso (and a few doggy biscuits for puppy) can be a great way to socialize your dog if you can find a nice outdoor café. Let the puppy sit outside with you while you enjoy your favorite coffee or tea. Many people will approach you and say hi to the puppy, and these encounters will give your puppy the chance to see different types of people, hear different voices, and get lots of attention. The more people who meet your puppy, the better. Your puppy will also be able to watch passersby and the goings-on at the café and around him on the street, which give him wonderful exposure to new stimuli.

When you take your puppy for walks through town, it is important to encourage him to walk on different surfaces, especially those that may frighten him. For example, if you approach a grate in the sidewalk, your puppy may refuse to step on it. Some indoor surfaces, such as slippery marble floors, can also be scary at first. If your puppy hesitates to walk on such surfaces, walk along with him, encouraging him to accompany you with a treat. When he sees you walking on the sidewalk grate or marble floor, he will feel safe in doing the same.

THERAPY DOGS

Names like "Love on a Leash" and "Angel on a Leash" well describe the work that therapy dogs do in our communities. A dog's love is neither conditional nor limited—there's plenty to go around, well beyond the walls of your home. Your well-socialized dog, with some basic training, may be ideal as a therapy dog if he has a steady, happy personality and the desire to be around people. Therapy dogs visit nursing homes, hospice centers, hospitals, and rehabilitation facilities to bring companionship and happiness to the patients and residents. These visits lift the spirits of those in hospitals and therapeutic settings and can even help expedite their recovery in some cases.

The American Kennel Club's Therapy Dog Program rewards owners who have taken the time to train and certify their dogs as therapy dogs and who go on regular visits with their dogs. In order to earn the Therapy Dog (THD) title, you and your AKC-registered or -listed dog must be certified/registered by an AKC-recognized therapy dog organization and perform a minimum of fifty visits. Both purebred and mixed-breed dogs qualify to participate in this program.

Therapy dog organizations provide training classes and evaluations for dogs and their owners with the goal of therapy dog certification. Therapy dogs must demonstrate reliable knowledge of basic obedience commands and behave properly around other people, around other dogs, and in new situations; in fact, most therapy dog organizations require dogs to have the AKC's Canine Good Citizen® certification as a prerequisite to becoming approved as therapy dogs. Therapy dogs must not be startled by people who walk differently, are in wheelchairs, or use IV poles or other types of medical equipment. All of your puppy socialization you will pay off when, as an adult, your dog can adapt to the different people he meets and the activities of healthcare facilities with ease and is well behaved around the other therapy dogs and their owners.

To find out more about getting your dog registered as a therapy dog, contact one of the approximately 100 organizations that work with the AKC, such as Bright and Beautiful Therapy Dogs, Pet Partners (formerly Delta Society), Love on a Leash, Therapy Dogs Incorporated (TD Inc.), and Therapy Dogs International (TDI).

Getting Used to Noises

Dogs don't really like rock and roll. Given a choice, dogs prefer a quiet, undisturbed environment. We often don't give a thought to how noisy our own homes are, with appliances buzzing, music blaring, and cell phones and doorbells ringing. Your puppy will need to get used to different sounds around the house. Dogs can be frightened by simple things such as doors slamming shut, the vacuum cleaner, the coffee grinder, the dishwasher, and the garbage disposal. Even a football game or a loud commercial on TV can startle a dog if he is not used to it. Be sure to expose your puppy to all of these sounds. Do not make an issue out of it—just turn on the television or vacuum cleaner when he is nearby and let him hear the noises that they make. The more he hears these sounds, the less likely he is to be frightened by them.

Your canine pal can do a lot with you as long as you take proper safety measures, such as this seafarer's harness and life vest.

When walking your puppy, don't avoid the noisy places in town. Walk him near construction sites, near hospitals, and on the sidewalk along busy streets. You want your puppy to hear and become desensitized to all sorts of noises, such as the loud wail of a siren and the roar of a truck speeding by, that could frighten him later in life if he grows up without being exposed and accustomed to them.

Flight Instinct

The flight instinct period takes place usually between four and eight months of age and is the beginning of a puppy's adolescence. During this time, it will likely seem as if your puppy has forgotten all of his previous training. He may begin to ignore you when you call him and try to grab forbidden objects to see if you will chase him. He is testing the boundaries of your rules.

At this stage, it is important to increase your obedience training and maintain a strict routine, possibly even stricter than in the past. Do not give your puppy as much freedom as you used to; instead, keep the puppy close to you and on his leash so that he can't run off as his independence and curiosity increase. As he becomes more independent, your puppy feels that he doesn't need to take as much direction from you, and that feeling will be reinforced if you, as pack leader, do not follow through and ensure that he follows the rules. This is the time that your puppy will test you more and more; if you are not careful, the nature of your relationship will change, and he will become the one in charge.

IMPORTANT PUPPY MILESTONES

Over the years, many behaviorists have purported their theories on the developmental stages of puppies. The following philosophy is indebted to Clarence Pfaffenberger's *New Knowledge of Dog Behavior* and Steven R. Lindsay's *Handbook of Applied Animal Behavior*.

NEONATAL PERIOD— BIRTH TO TWELVE DAYS:

At this beginning stage of life, puppies don't see or hear very well. They respond to touch, and they stick close to their mother. They find their mother's nipples with their sense of smell and by feeling her warmth. At this stage, puppies are unable to regulate their body temperatures and their elimination. Their mother keeps them clean when they urinate or defecate.

When a young puppy experiences mild stress at this young age, it actually increases the puppy's brain size and causes a hormonal reaction in the adrenal system that increases the strength of the immune system. This strengthens the puppy's ability to be resilient during challenging times throughout his life and enables him to learn more quickly and easily.

When visiting a breeder and looking at the puppies, ask about the stressors to which the pups have been exposed. At this stage, simply moving a puppy away from his mother so that he has to work harder to get back to her is a stressor.

Music playing in the background or lights being turned on and off can also create some stress for the litter. Pinching the puppies' feet or holding the puppies on their backs very gently are other stress exercises that the breeder may practice.

TRANSITIONAL PERIOD— THIRTEEN TO TWENTY DAYS:

The puppies are starting to move around, albeit not very well; they fall over often. At this time, the breeder may introduce the litter to stimuli such as towels and cardboard boxes. The breeder should be picking the puppies up, touching them, and talking to them. Although their sight and hearing are limited, their eyes and ears start to open, and they begin to respond to taste. They begin to wag their tails and start to gain some control over their bodily functions.

AWARENESS PERIOD— TWENTY-ONE TO TWENTY-THREE DAYS:

During this time, there is marked improvement in sight and hearing. The need for a stable environment is of utmost importance at this time. During this period, the breeder must not make any sudden changes in the whelping-box environment. The puppies' area needs to remain in the same location, and the puppies need to be close to their mother and littermates.

Playing soft background music and introducing the pups to different types of surfaces under their feet, such as carpet, linoleum, and concrete, are helpful to the social development of the puppies.

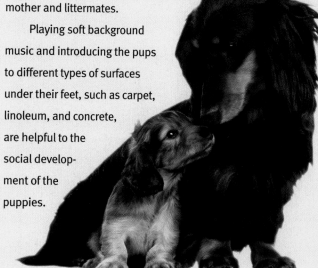

CANINE SOCIALIZATION— TWENTY-ONE TO FORTY-NINE DAYS:

Socialization among the litter is at its peak during this phase. The puppies learn proper bite inhibition, to accept discipline from their mother, and to interact appropriately with their littermates. This is the time when puppies learn the most about how to play with other canines. A puppy who is removed from his litter or mother during this time will miss out on important life lessons, which will create problems later in his interactions with other dogs and animals.

The breeder may start early house-training during this period by placing an exercise pen next to the whelping box so that the puppies can relieve themselves in the exercise pen and sleep and play in the whelping box. They should be learning that their potty area is different from their sleeping, eating, and playing area. The breeder must keep the puppies' areas clean so that the puppies do not learn to participate in coprophagia (feces eating).

Short-term isolation from the litter is a wise idea at this age. The breeder can take one or two puppies out at a time for very brief car rides so that they get used to being apart from their littermates and get to see new sights, hear different sounds, and smell different scents. The puppies have been learning about canine behavior from their mother and littermates, but they also need to be aware of the differences between canine and human societies.

This is also a critical time for the breeder to spend time with the puppies, interacting with, touching, holding, and cuddling them. This attention increases their touch tolerance, their capacity for learning, and their confidence.

HUMAN SOCIALIZATION— SEVEN TO TWELVE WEEKS:

The best time for puppies to go to their new homes is during this time period. Your puppy is most receptive to meeting new people at this age, so aim to introduce him to as many new people as possible. Sit outside at a local coffee shop and let anyone who's interested pet the puppy.

This is the time to start training for short periods of time. Studies have consistently shown that early training makes dogs brighter, happier, healthier, more willing to please, and less likely to develop problem behaviors. At this age, the puppy has the ability to acknowledge you as his pack leader, learn by association, and respond to simple behavioral cues such as *sit*, *stay*, and *come*. Permanent human/dog bonding begins, and the puppy is able to accept gentle corrections and develop confidence in himself. House-training also begins at this time and should start as soon as puppy comes home.

FEAR IMPRINT PERIOD— EIGHT TO ELEVEN WEEKS:

This is a precarious time during which it is important that nothing really scares your puppy. As the puppy's owner, you need to do all you can to ensure that the puppy is happy, confident, and not too startled or frightened by anything. This is not the time to take your puppy to the dog park to meet large, overly playful dogs. Any children who meet your puppy need to handle him very gently. The puppy's assumptions about the world and reactions to his environment become very permanent at this stage.

SENIORITY CLASSIFICATION—
TEN TO SIXTEEN WEEKS:

This critical period is also known as the "age of cutting"—cutting teeth and cutting apron strings. At this age, the puppy begins testing your dominance and leadership. Keep the puppy on leash at all times when he is free inside the house so that you have the opportunity to stop him from getting into trouble or correct him when he does something that you don't want him to do.

If your puppy starts nipping and biting at you, correct him every single time. If he is not taught otherwise at this age, he will always be a mouther, which becomes very annoying. When your puppy puts his mouth on you, say "Ouch!" and stop playing until he calms down. When he stops, give him a lot of praise.

Your puppy is becoming a bit more independent and may start testing his boundaries and his role in the pack. If you notice that your puppy is already showing signs of dominance or stubbornness at this stage, it must be addressed immediately with the help of a professional trainer, as this is not something that he will outgrow. In fact, puppies who show signs of dominance, stubbornness, or aggression at this age will become much bolder in the coming months, especially during adolescence.

FLIGHT INSTINCT PERIOD—
FOUR TO EIGHT MONTHS:

This period is, in essence, early adolescence, similar to that of a human preteen. Your puppy doesn't come when called as eagerly as he once did. He doesn't play fetch as much anymore. He may be uncomfortable if his adult teeth are coming in. Obedience classes are a must for your preteen puppy. You will head off destructive behavior and reinforce that you are the boss as your puppy starts to challenge your role as pack leader. Obedience training challenges the puppy physically as he performs cues, and it challenges him mentally by teaching him to think and learn. Training gives a puppy a psychological advantage because as he is taught his place in the pack, he's also gaining confidence and learning right from wrong.

SECOND FEAR PERIOD—
SIX TO FOURTEEN MONTHS

This stage occurs in conjunction with adolescence and sexual maturity. During this time, the puppy reaches his full adult height but will continue to fill out. The age at which you have your puppy spayed or neutered will determine how much he fills out; if the surgery is done around six months, the puppy will have a more adolescent body, and if you wait until he is older to have him altered, he will fill out more as an adult.

At this stage, your puppy has learned that he can romp as he pleases, or so he thinks. He wants to explore and is not as dependent upon you as he once was. If you have not yet enrolled in a training class with your puppy, now is the time. This is your puppy's "rebellious teenager" phase, and if you are not firm with him when problems occur, you will only have bigger problems later on in his life.

CHAPTER 4

House-Training Your Puppy

House-training a puppy is surprisingly similar to potty-training a toddler, minus the diapers. Heidi Murkoff, one of the authors of the *What to Expect* series of parenting books, offers some good commonsense "dos" and "don'ts" that apply here, such as "Do watch closely," "Do offer praise," "Don't expect too much too soon," "Don't scold, punish, or shame," and "Don't lose hope." As frustrating and time-consuming as house-training a puppy may be, our canine young ones master good bathroom habits much faster and at a much younger age than a human toddler does. By the time your puppy is two years old, not only is he house-trained, he could be an Obedience Trial Champion!

People are sometimes confused about how to get started with a young puppy. If you start training your puppy to relieve himself on puppy pads indoors, but you intend to start taking the puppy outdoors for potty trips when he gets older, you are just confusing your puppy and creating a problem for yourself in the future. Decide from the outset whether you want your dog to be pad-trained for the rest

of his life or trained to go to the bathroom outside. Whatever you decide, be prepared to start on Day One and have all of the necessary supplies on hand.

The benefits of house-training your dog to relieve himself outside are many. You won't have the expense of purchasing pads for the rest of the dog's life. You'll have a reason to walk your dog on a regular basis. You won't have to worry about the smell of soiled puppy pads. If you visit friends' or relatives' homes with your dog, the chances are slim that he will have an accident indoors, as he knows only to go to the bathroom outside. One drawback is that you will have to take your dog outdoors in bad weather if you don't have a fenced-in yard in which you can let him out safely; your dog may even refuse to go outdoors in bad weather. Further, pad-training may be feasible for small-breed dogs throughout their lives, but it doesn't work well with larger dogs as they reach adolescence and adulthood.

The benefits to pad-training are that your dog will always have a place to relieve himself no matter the weather. Your dog will remain cleaner and is less likely to be exposed to parasites from other dogs than if he relieves himself in public places. A downside to pad-training is that when you visit someone else's home and don't put a pad down for your dog right away, he is likely to have an accident indoors. Pad-training is also expensive—the pads are not cheap, and you will have to remember to purchase them regularly. You may choose to use newspaper instead, but wet newspaper can create an unpleasant odor in the home, as can pads if they are not changed frequently. Plus, your dog's indoor potty area may take up a bit of room.

For some people, particularly city dwellers or owners of small dogs, pad- or paper-training is the most convenient way to house-train.

Many people want to train their dogs to both use pads and go outdoors; however, when you do that, it is very difficult for the dog to decipher where he is supposed to go to the bathroom. It is like teaching a child that he is supposed to go on the toilet, but he can just go in his diaper when it is more convenient. It is a confusing concept for a young dog.

The bottom line, whatever your situation, is that the sooner you establish the puppy's habit of going to the bathroom where you want him to, be it outdoors or on pads, the better. It cannot be emphasized enough that you must stick with one method and be consistent.

What's Great about Crates!

If you decide to train your dog to relieve himself outdoors, you'll find it very helpful to crate-train him. The first thing you will need, of course, is a crate. There are people who want to house-train but don't want to use a crate, but the crate-training method makes it an easier and more

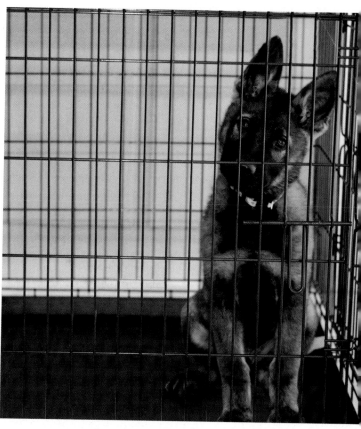

Before your puppy is house-trained, don't line the crate with towels, blankets, papers, or anything else he may soil.

efficient process. The crate teaches a puppy to "hold it" for short periods of time and will keep him from relieving himself in inappropriate places because he instinctually wants to keep his den area clean. It also gives the puppy a safe space to which he can retreat when he needs some quiet time.

Try feeding your puppy inside the crate at first so that he associates the crate with good things; also keep a few of his toys in the crate for comfort and entertainment. Do not put any blankets in the crate at first. It is important to let the puppy get used to the bare bottom of the crate; it will keep him cool and he will become very comfortable in it. If you keep a blanket or towel in the crate, the puppy will learn that he can go to the bathroom on it and then just push it to the side so he still has a clean area to rest on. He will learn just the opposite of what you want—that it is okay to go inside the crate.

First thing in the morning, release your puppy from the crate and take him directly outside on leash. During the first week, you may want to pick him up and carry him outside so he doesn't get the chance to have an accident in the house. As he sniffs around, give him a verbal cue such as "Go potty" or "Do your business." Stay outside for only five to seven minutes. If he goes to the bathroom during that time, let him run around the house for fifteen to twenty minutes when you go back inside. If he does not relieve himself, return him to the crate. This is not a punishment; rather, you are simply taking away the opportunity for him to go to the bathroom in the house.

BARKING IN THE CRATE

If your puppy starts barking when you put him in his crate, ignore him and walk away. If you let the puppy out every time he barks, he will learn that he doesn't have to stay in the crate and that all he has to do to get out is make a little noise.

You want to be persistent and consistent about discouraging barking in the crate so that your puppy learns that barking will not be tolerated. He will not become aggressive or begin to dislike you if you do this; rather, he will learn that incessant barking does not get him the attention he is seeking. It is simple—and it's the small things like this that help develop balance in your relationship with your dog.

Thirty minutes later, take the puppy outside again. Remember, he's out there to do his business, not sniff the trees and chase the birds, but he may need a little activity, such as a short, brisk walk, to get him to go potty. If he goes, he gets fifteen to twenty minutes of free time in the house; if not, he goes back into the crate. Repeat this every two to three hours.

When you leave the house, take the puppy outside right before you leave and then return him to the crate. It is important to do this whether you are running a quick errand or leaving for several hours, although initially you should not leave the puppy alone for more than two or three hours. When you come home, take the puppy outside immediately. In the evening, feed your puppy his dinner about four hours before bedtime. For the puppy's last trip outside before he goes into the crate for the night, take him on a fifteen- to twenty-minute walk. A nice brisk walk will give him the opportunity to empty himself before he goes to sleep.

If your puppy has an accident, and you've been taking him out every three hours, go back to every two hours and give him shorter periods of free time. This is not a punishment, and your dog will not perceive it as such; you are just trying to help him succeed.

The logic behind crate-training is that a dog will not want to soil his den, the area where he sleeps. If you have a dog who goes to the bathroom in his crate, you may have a dog with "dirty dog syndrome," and you'll

When your puppy is accustomed to his crate as his own special place, he will naturally try to keep it clean.

Don't let your puppy get distracted during potty trips outside. He can be rewarded with free time once he does his business.

need to reverse the house-training process to correct the problem. If you have a backyard, instead of keeping the puppy crated for periods of time and then giving him free time once he goes to the bathroom, you will want to keep him outside longer, making sure that he relieves himself during your time outdoors. Once he has relieved himself outside, put him in his crate for half an hour at a time so that he learns to keep the crate clean.

GUIDELINES FOR OUTDOOR POTTY VISITS

Up to four months old .... Every two to three hours
Four to six months old .... Every three to four hours
Six to nine months old .... Every four to six hours

Puppies older than nine months can hold it for up to eight hours but should of course be taken out more frequently when someone is home. Many dog owners who work during the day opt to come home at lunchtime to give their dogs midday breaks for potty time and exercise. If you cannot come home during the day, consider asking a friendly neighbor to visit your puppy or investing in a dog walker.

If your puppy habitually soils his crate and you don't have a backyard, you will need to keep your puppy attached to you (for example, by attaching the handle of his leash to your belt loop) so that he cannot leave your side. This way, he cannot sneak off and go to the bathroom somewhere in the house, and he also will not dirty himself and his crate. Take him outside for short walks every hour to hour and a half. Walk him, and if he goes to the bathroom, bring him inside and put him in his crate for about five minutes. When you release him from the crate, attach him

Be observant! When you see your puppy searching for a spot, you'll know it's time to get him outside right away.

to you again. You should also feed him his meals inside the crate during this process. All of these things are teaching him to keep his crate clean; if the problem persists, you may need the help of a professional trainer.

Some owners don't want to keep their dogs in crates for extended periods of time when someone is at home. In this case, put your puppy's leash on and attach the handle to your belt loop to keep the puppy close to you as described in the previous paragraphs. Stick to the schedule of taking him outside every couple of hours, and pay attention to his body language when you're back in the house—most likely, you'll know if he is going to have an accident before he does, and you'll be able to get him outside again right away.

It is important to use the crate for at least the first year of your puppy's life, even if only for bedtime and when no one is home. You do not want to make the mistake of suddenly giving your

HOUSE-TRAINING SCHEDULE

FIRST THING IN THE MORNING: Take the puppy out for a short walk. Bring him inside and feed him in his crate; leave the food down for about ten minutes and then remove it.

THIRTY MINUTES LATER: Take the puppy out to relieve himself.

EVERY TWO HOURS THEREAFTER: Take the puppy outside to relieve himself. If he goes during that time, go back inside for fifteen minutes of free time. If he doesn't go, return him to his crate for thirty minutes and then take him out again.

DINNERTIME: Feed your puppy inside the crate; remove the food after about ten minutes.

THIRTY MINUTES LATER: Take the puppy out for a short walk. If he relieves himself, give him twenty minutes of free time indoors. If he doesn't go, return him to the crate.

TWO HOURS LATER: Take the puppy out for another short walk. If he relieves himself, give him twenty minutes of free time indoors. If he doesn't go, return him to the crate and try again before bedtime.

IMMEDIATELY BEFORE BEDTIME: Take the puppy out for a brisk walk and make sure that he relieves himself.

If you are diligent and consistent with this schedule, and you praise your puppy when he goes in his spot, he will quickly learn to go to the bathroom during his short periods of time outdoors. After about two weeks of following this schedule, your puppy should be getting the hang of it, and you can start taking him out every four hours and rewarding him with limited amounts of free time after he relieves himself.

puppy full run of the house while you are sleeping or not home. Build up his freedom gradually as he becomes more reliable with his house-training; for example, if he's usually crated overnight in your bedroom, let him sleep out of the crate with your bedroom door closed. Next, let him sleep out of the crate in your bedroom with the bedroom door open, but use gates to block his access to other rooms. As he does fine with more and more freedom, keep expanding his area little by little.

Indoor Training

If you have chosen to train your dog to use puppy pads indoors, start by finding a suitable area, such as a small bathroom, to be his potty area. Place pads on the floor in the corner. Pick a spot in the room for your puppy's bed as well as for his food and water; this way, he has specific places to lie down, eat, and drink, and he is limited to going to the bathroom only on the pads. Keep a baby gate across the doorway so that it is impossible for the puppy leave the area and go to the bathroom somewhere else. Using this strategy, you set the dog up for success by limiting the chances that he will have accidents.

This padded area will become the puppy's primary turf for the entire potty-training process. He will play, eat, drink, and sleep in this area. Each morning, check right away to see if the puppy went to the bathroom. If he did, pick up the soiled pad and put down a clean one. If you know that he has gone in the last few minutes, you can let him run around the house for about fifteen minutes and then put him back into the padded area. Each time he goes to the bathroom on the pads, replace the dirty ones with clean ones and give him fifteen minutes of free time. If you are regularly gone for hours each day, you should initially have a dog walker come to check on the puppy, clean up any dirty pads, and spend some time playing with the puppy to give him some exercise.

After a week of success, make the potty area smaller by removing one of the pads. After each subsequent accident-free week, remove another one of the pads and increase the amount of puppy's free time in fifteen-minute increments. Removing the pads will give the puppy a smaller area on which to relieve himself while keeping the same area for rest and eating plus a new area of bare floor. If your puppy has an accident, meaning that he goes to the bathroom where there is no pad, go back a step and enlarge the potty area by one pad.

When you see your dog circling around on the padding, looking for a spot, it is a good idea to repeatedly issue a verbal cue such as "Go potty" or "Do your business." Reward the pup with attention, praise, and free time when you see him relieve himself in the correct spot. As your puppy continues to progress in his training, give him more frequent periods of free time, not just longer periods of free time.

When the puppy is using just one pad in his confined area, you can be confident that the puppy understands that he is to go on the pad and only on the pad. At this point, you can give him more freedom and place pads in different parts of the house. Increase his freedom little by little; for example, open up new sections of the house one room at a time. Put up baby gates and close doors so that he doesn't have access to the entire house all at once.

Accidents happen! Learn to read your puppy's body language so you can prevent mishaps in the house.

CHAPTER 5

First Lessons for the Young Dog

Take out your lesson planner and get ready for homeschooling! The first days of lessons for your puppy are a bit like nursery school for children— all about fun and some basic skills. We won't be teaching your puppy the colors of the rainbow and the letters of the alphabet, but we will be working on fetching and chasing and other fun playground activities.

When your puppy looks to you for affection, fun, and, of course, food, you quickly become his favorite person in the world. You're building a lasting bond with your puppy and cementing the pup's trust, so you must not do anything that will compromise that trust, such as harsh scolding or punishment. You will be setting some boundaries and rules for the pup, and praise and consistency build his trust in you.

Anything you do with your puppy sets patterns, teaches him lessons, and affects him for a lifetime. Play, exercise, and obedience sessions are all forms of training because you are teaching your puppy rules, setting limits,

Your puppy is just waiting to learn all that his new pack can teach him.

and, most importantly, showing him how to enjoy life. He is learning confidence and is challenged physically, mentally, and emotionally. When he is fulfilled in this way, he will be more at ease, you will be able to enjoy him more as a companion, and he will be less likely to behave inappropriately.

Fun Stuff: Balls and Other Toys

Balls that bounce and squeak and roll will captivate your young dog as he chases his "prey." Many dogs are natural retrievers, especially those who have been bred to retrieve, such as Labrador Retrievers and Golden Retrievers. However, a dog doesn't have to have generations of retrieving ability behind him to be a terrific retriever.

Start playtime by rolling a ball toward your puppy to pique his curiosity in the ball. Allow him to push it around, sniff it, paw at it, or play with it however he chooses. Once he shows interest in the ball, create a greater desire by taking it from him and rolling it away for him to chase after. When he does, clap your hands and act very excited, giving your puppy a lot of praise and affection.

Roll the ball away from your puppy again. Don't worry if he is not bringing it back to you at this point—just make it a lot of fun for him when he goes after the ball. Unless your puppy shows infinite enthusiasm for this game, keep it short. You don't want to push him too hard or cause him to become bored. Just spend a few minutes at a time playing ball with him.

If he picks up the ball in his mouth, give him a lot of praise and petting. Your dog considers petting a form of praise. Not all dogs enjoy hugs, but they do enjoy petting, so physical praise is just as important as verbal praise.

Sturdy rubber toys are great alternatives to balls. They come in different shapes and bounce unpredictably, providing mental stimulation for your puppy and adding excitement to your game.

Treat-dispensing toys are popular and come in different forms. You place small treats or pieces of dog food inside the toy, and the dog must figure out how to move the toy so that the treats are released. Some of these toys have holes in them, enabling treats to fall out as the dog rolls the toy around, while others release treats as the dog paws or noses different movable parts, such as small levers or doors.

Treat-dispensing toys are designed to satisfy a dog's chewing needs while also providing him with physical and mental exercise. These toys can keep some dogs amused

Playing together with toys allows your pup to expend some energy while you foster that essential dog/owner bond.

GROWING IN HIS SLEEP

Growing puppies need quiet time to sleep and rest. Everyone in the house, especially the kids, will want to play with the new puppy, but it is important that you don't allow anyone to overtire the new puppy or disturb him when he's in his crate. Just like babies, puppies need to rest so that they can grow and stay healthy and happy.

for quite a while; however, if a dog is not treat-driven or if the treats do not come out easily or consistently, the dog will become bored and frustrated and lose interest in the toy. Usually, owners must first show their dogs how to use this type of toy successfully.

Puppies with soft mouths will love plush squeaky toys, which come in all shapes, colors, and sizes. Having a "soft mouth" means that the dog doesn't bite down hard and is comfortable carrying something gently in his mouth. Sporting breeds usually have soft mouths because retrieving downed game without damaging it is one of the purposes for which they were developed.

Rubber chew toys have been popular for years. Some of these have raised bristles, which are intended to clean the dog's teeth as he chews. These toys are great for voracious chewers. They withstand hard biting and allow the puppy to explore using his mouth in a constructive way.

Recommended toys for a puppy include those that engage his mind as well as his mouth and those that can be used in interactive games with his owners.

Praise and More Praise!

When it comes to your puppy, you'll be giving praise every day! Of course, we're not talking about hymns and worship here, but rather ways to let your dog know that he's catching on to what you're teaching him or behaving the way that you want him to. The most popular form of praise is food rewards, which can be anything nutritious, bite-sized, and loved by your dog. Another effective way to praise your puppy is with love and affection in the form of joyful words and petting. A favorite stuffed or squeaky toy is also a great reward for a job well done. All dogs are different. Some work best for treats, some can't get enough belly rubs, and some prefer playtime with that much-loved plush giraffe.

The advantages of using treats as rewards in training are that they are small, they are easy to carry, and just about any dog will eat a treat if it's something that he likes. The drawbacks are that treats can be messy, a dog may not eat a treat if he is not hungry, and not all dogs are food-motivated.

Hands-on attention and your praise are valuable rewards for your dog.

Love, happy words, and petting are things that you always have handy, and you don't need an extra hand or a pocket to carry them. Lavishing praise will likely get your pup to roll over for belly rubs, which most dogs love and will work for. Throwing his favorite toy around rewards him with playtime with his favorite person.

Bonding with Your Puppy

You don't need a self-help book to find the right way to love your dog. From the day you first saw your puppy, showing him affection very likely came naturally. For most of us, it's puppy love at first sight! Puppies respond to petting, cuddling, and all kinds of attention, but bonding goes beyond that to everyday activities such as feeding, walking, talking, socializing, and, of course, training.

Like children, dogs hate to be ignored, so the more attention you can lavish on your puppy, the happier he will be. Dogs are abundantly generous, naturally social creatures who have evolved to work with, live with, play with, and love humans. Anything that you do with your puppy, whether it is playtime, snuggle time, or training time, helps strengthen your bond with him. Your puppy will bond with all of the people who care for him, feed him, take him for walks, play with him, and train him.

Setting the Rules

A human needs to be the one to set boundaries for the new puppy and establish what behaviors are acceptable in the house. These rules must be firm, fair, and consistent, and the puppy should be rewarded whenever he follows them.

Don't underestimate the value of just plain fun in building your bond with your puppy.

Rules are fair if the puppy is taught what to do and what not to do. Consistency happens when the rules are clear and enforced the same way, all the time, by everyone in the household. Rules become unfair if you don't always stick to them, meaning that you allow certain behaviors sometimes but correct the puppy for those same behaviors at other times.

When you train your puppy to sit and stay at the front door, don't make a big deal about it if he breaks the *sit/stay* before you release him. Instead, simply walk up to the puppy and put him back into the *sit/stay* position. When your dog does the right thing (for example, he sits and stays at the front door until you tell him he can walk through), you express that you are pleased with him through verbal praise and the look of pleasure on your face. He will be proud of himself because he knows that he has done his job well. After learning a few lessons like this, he will realize that doing the right thing brings positive responses and doing the wrong thing brings consequences. This is the most fair and most efficient way to teach a dog the difference between right and wrong.

Time Out, Puppy!

A brief "time out," the popular psychology approach to defusing children's bad behavior, can be effective for wound-up, naughty puppies. Dogs live in the moment, and while experts disagree about how much dogs actually remember, most trainers agree that if you scold a puppy after the fact for urinating on the carpet, it does no good because he will not know what he's being punished for.

When a trainer tells a puppy owner to put the puppy in his crate after he's had a potty accident, it is not as a means of punishment; rather, it is intended to take away the puppy's opportunity to have another accident in the house. The same is true when the puppy is getting into things that he shouldn't or trying to chew on forbidden objects during his free time around the house. By putting the puppy in the crate very calmly, you are simply giving him some time to rest. This is essentially setting the puppy up to succeed. If you put the puppy in his crate at regular intervals for house-training, for feeding times,

DIRECT SUPERVISION

The crate is the perfect place for keeping your puppy out of mischief when you are not able to watch him or when you are not at home. It is never a good idea to give the puppy the run of the house without direct supervision. Direct supervision means that the puppy is in the same room as you are at all times. Invest in baby gates so that you can block the puppy's access to certain parts of your house. Be sure to keep an eye on him during his free time in the house or yard.

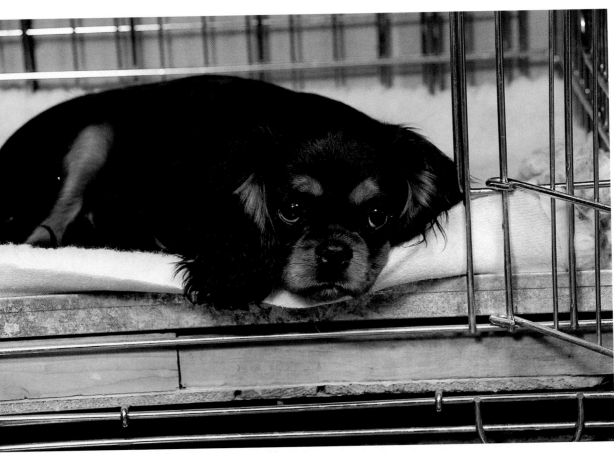

Once your dog is accustomed to his crate, he'll likely go into it on his own when he needs a little down time.

for naps and bedtime, and to keep him out of trouble, he will consider the crate as a safe haven and not as a place of punishment.

Training is all about timing. You have to be there to correct your puppy at the moment he does something wrong. As an example, by attaching your puppy's leash to his collar during his free time in the house, you can teach the puppy when he's doing something wrong by simply reaching out for the leash, giving the leash a little tug to get his attention, and telling him "No."

Never hit, yell at, throw things at, or scold the puppy in any manner. That is *not* a correction. If you are out of control (and you are if you behave like this), your puppy also will be out of control. Treating your puppy this way only hurts your bond with your dog, causing mistrust and possibly fear and aggression.

Classes and Trainers

While homeschooling makes a great beginning, puppy classes are a great way to improve your understanding of canine behavior and to socialize your puppy. Important socialization begins with the puppy's littermates and should continue when you bring your puppy home with you. Up to sixteen weeks of age is a perfect time to reap the socialization benefits that a puppy class provides. It is imperative that you discuss this with your veterinarian, as you want to make sure that he or she feels that your puppy is sufficiently vaccinated to be around other young puppies. It is important to get clearance from your veterinarian before enrolling in a class.

If you are having potty issues with the new puppy, think about hiring a private trainer for at least one session to get on track with house-training. If you have not made significant progress by the time the puppy is four months old, seek help from a professional trainer.

When it comes to working with a trainer for obedience lessons, you can choose between group classes and private training. Group classes are more affordable and are usually scheduled in the evenings. These classes are good for socialization and basic lessons, but if your dog has specific issues, they may not be addressed in a group class because there's not as much opportunity for one-on-one attention from the trainer. Private training is nice because the sessions are scheduled when it is convenient for you,

All of the training you do, whether at home, in a class, or both, pays off as your puppy grows into a reliable and enjoyable companion.

Puppy classes give you a foundation in basic obedience exercises so you can practice at home.

and the training is tailored to your dog and his needs. These sessions can be held in your home, at a training school, or even in public places, such as a local park or another public area where you live, so that your dog can learn to behave in a variety of environments. Sessions with a private trainer in your home tend to be more expensive initially, but you can often accomplish more in less time. Private sessions at a training school are often a less expensive option because you are saving the trainer the travel time.

One of the first questions most owners ask trainers is, "How much do lessons cost?" The best question to ask, however, is, "In your course, what can I expect—and not expect—to accomplish with my dog?" You need to know about a trainer's experience, methods, and of course fees, but you first need to find out the trainer's goals before you spend your money. More experienced trainers are often more effective, so although their per-lesson fee is higher, you may ultimately save money in the long run by needing fewer lessons. However, keep in mind that the most expensive trainer is not always the best, and someone with lower rates may be just as good. Again, the best question you can ask any instructor before hiring him or her is, "What can I expect from my dog after training?"

It is important to get recommendations before hiring a trainer or enrolling in a training class; your veterinarian and other puppy owners can be good resources. For well-run, cost-effective, and results-oriented group classes, contact one of the American Kennel Club's obedience clubs; you can search the AKC's website (www.akc.org) for clubs in your area. You can also find experienced trainers for your puppy via the AKC S.T.A.R. Puppy® and Canine Good Citizen® evaluator list at www.akc.org/events/cgc/cgc_bystate.cfm.

The Name Game and *Watch*

Let's begin with the most basic lesson of all: teaching the puppy his name. This simple exercise is the first step to calling your puppy and retaining his attention, but first, of course, you have to pick a name. Choose a name that is short and easy—one that doesn't sound too similar to typical commands or to the name of someone in the house. Keep in mind that the name you choose for your dog will affect people's perception of him as well as reflect upon you as an owner. For example, a dog named Cujo will become the most feared dog on the block even if he is a cuddly sweetheart.

You may want to try a few names out, each for a day or two, before you make a final decision. For example, your first choice might be Barkley, but you discover after your

Teaching your puppy to respond to his name also lays the foundation for the *come* cue.

puppy is home with you for a few days that he's really your Buddy. Another common practice is to give your dog a name befitting his breed's country of origin, such as Seamus for a Soft Coated Wheaten Terrier, Fritz for a German Shepherd Dog, or Coco for a French Bulldog. Whatever you choose to name your dog, make sure that it is simple, that it is easy to say, and that everyone in the family likes it.

To teach your puppy to respond to his name, just keep using it. Each time he looks at you when you say his name, give him a treat and lots of love. Next, stand in front of him while he is on leash, point to your eyes, and say "Watch." Praise him as long as he keeps his eyes on you—"Good dog, watch me. That's good, watch. Watch me." When he starts to look away, turn around and walk in the opposite direction, still holding the leash. This may confuse him at first, but it teaches him that if he looks away from you, you are going to leave his side (although he will still be attached to you). He will learn quite quickly that he has to keep watching you for you to stay nearby. Do not say the puppy's name when you give the *watch* cue; you want him to learn the word and respond to the cue, not respond because you used his name.

You can practice the *watch* cue in many instances throughout the day, such as when you take your puppy outside for a walk or when you're working on other obedience cues. In a week, you will have a dog who is always watching you.

Walking on Leash

There is nothing fun about being tugged down the sidewalk by a hyperactive adolescent dog. Walking your dog can be a fun, rejuvenating activity for both of you, so mastering this lesson will give you hours of pleasure in the years to come. Teaching your new puppy how to walk on leash without pulling also strengthens your bond with your dog and sets the stage for future training. This beginning lesson trains your puppy to look to you for direction, teaches you how to take the role of leader, and develops a relationship built on love and discipline. Leash training also stimulates and exercises your puppy on mental, physical, and psychological levels—mental because it teaches your puppy to pay attention to you for direction, physical because he is walking and learning to be aware of your pace so

The first step of on-leash walking is making sure that your puppy is comfortable with his leash on.

Your dog should start off on your left side before the two of you begin moving forward.

that he moves his body at the same speed, and psychological because he is learning that you are the one in charge.

Begin with the leash in your right hand and your puppy at your left side. It may seem counterintuitive to hold the leash across your body; however, it is important to develop good habits from the start. It's easy to hold the leash too tightly if it's in your left hand, especially as your puppy matures. When you have the leash in your right hand and let it hang across your body, there will be slack (no tension) in the leash, which is what you want.

Place the thumb of your right hand through the loop of the leash and relax your arm at your side. As you move forward, keeping the puppy on your left side, tell him "Let's go" in an upbeat voice. Whatever verbal cue you use, always use the same one and always keep a happy tone of voice.

As you move forward, use your verbal cue along with encouraging words: "Let's go! That's a good puppy." If your puppy should stop, tell him "Let's walk" and start walking again. If you have a small-breed puppy, you can be very tempted to just pick him up and carry him if he's not walking the way you want him to, but this will start a habit that is very difficult to break, and it teaches the puppy that he doesn't have to walk if he doesn't want to. Why should he walk if you're going to pick him up and carry him instead? Carrying your puppy everywhere encourages laziness and teaches him that he is the one in charge.

When walking (or teaching any command), getting the puppy's attention makes all the difference, but you might need the assistance of some tasty liver or chicken to keep his attention. Many trainers incorporate treats into the walking lesson. Find out which food treat is your puppy's favorite, which is likely something soft and yummy (and smelly!). Once you figure out which treat really gets his instant attention, you know you've found your training tool. Likewise, you might use a toy that he truly flips over.

Once the puppy is in place and ready to walk, lean over and let him smell the treat in your hand. Do not give him any of it, not even a lick. Now you have his attention. If you're using a clicker (see "Clicker Training" in chapter 8), you can click (or make a clicking or popping noise with your mouth to get his attention). As you step out with your puppy following you (dangling a smelly hand at his nose level), click as he walks at your side and give him a nibble of the treat. This positive-training method teaches the puppy that walking along with you is a good thing and pays off in his favorite treat (or toy).

If your puppy is a bit stubborn on the leash, he may plant his feet and refuse to move. Just say "Let's go" and start walking. If you have to give another little tug on the leash and say "Let's go" again, it's okay to do so. After two or three tries, the puppy should give in and walk with you; however, if he is extra stubborn, you may have to crouch down and tell him "Come here." As he starts to move toward you, turn and start moving forward with him so that he ends up joining you on your left-hand side—and before he knows it, he's walking along with you. Once he's walking with you, keep moving and don't stop.

Practice your puppy's on-leash walking by going back and forth for a short distance several times. Once the puppy is consistently walking on leash politely, he may be ready to improve his technique, and you can teach him what we call an *about turn*. Here's how it's done: When you turn to walk back the way you came, turn to your right. It is important to walk back and forth at first, incorporating about turns rather than just taking long walks, when teaching your puppy to heel. Frequent turns teach the puppy to pay close attention to you and walk at your pace. When you take a long walk, it is easy for you and your puppy to become distracted, and your pup learns to stop at every fire hydrant or lunge toward every squirrel he sees. It's also easier on a long walk for your puppy to walk too far out on your left side. By teaching him in short walks, you can pay closer attention and keep the puppy at your left side.

If your puppy has a tendency to run ahead of you, stop, do an about turn, and immediately walk in the opposite direction. This accomplishes two things: first, it slows the puppy down; second, it teaches the puppy to pay attention to you and where you are going. Each time he runs ahead of you, he becomes distracted and loses focus. However, if you keep turning around unexpectedly, he will learn very quickly to watch where you are going because you keep changing course on him without warning.

The AKC S.T.A.R. Puppy® Program

The AKC is a huge proponent of responsible pet ownership; to that end, it developed the AKC S.T.A.R. Puppy® Program. The AKC S.T.A.R. Puppy Program is designed to inspire all owners of purebred and mixed-breed dogs to train their puppies and create balanced, healthy, and happy relationships with them that will last throughout their dogs' lives. The program is also designed to educate owners on puppy-raising issues and how to be proactive dog owners.

AKC S.T.A.R. Puppy is a non-competitive activity that is open to all dogs under one year of age and their owners. It is the starting point for any owner who wants his or her puppy to go on to train for and receive the AKC's Canine Good Citizen (CGC) certification, which can open doors to competitive sports, such as rally and obedience, as well as therapy-dog training.

S.T.A.R. stands for **s**ocialization, **t**raining, **a**ctivity, and **r**esponsibility, which are key components in the type of lifelong relationship you want to cultivate with your dog. The first part of the program is a six-week-long puppy training class taught by an AKC CGC evaluator. The course socializes your puppy so that he can become a well-adjusted member of society. It trains him in the basic cues, such as to come when called and to sit and stay, and it shows you how to teach, practice, and reinforce these cues on your own. It encourages and teaches you how to best exercise your puppy so that he is challenged and fulfilled mentally and physically. It educates you about responsible dog ownership and etiquette in the community and teaches you how to provide proactive care, such as health care and grooming, at all stages of your dog's life.

One of the first cues you'll teach your puppy is *sit*, which forms the basis for more advanced exercises.

You and your puppy must attend all of the classes and complete the six-week course. At the last class, the instructor will administer the S.T.A.R. Puppy test. You will also be tested throughout the course on your responsibility as an owner. Your instructor will take notes each week about your preparedness for class. Do you bring clean-up bags for your puppy? Do you prepare and follow your weekly exercise plans for your puppy? Does your puppy always wear proper identification? You also want the instructor to see that your puppy is wearing an appropriate collar and is leashed at all times.

You will take the AKC's CGC Responsible Owner's Pledge, in which you vow to be responsible for your puppy's health, safety, good manners, and quality of life for his entire life. Health-care commitments include taking your dog to the veterinarian for regular visits, not just when he is sick; administering parasite preventives; and keeping up with grooming and good nutrition. Ensuring your dog's safety includes providing adequate fencing, not letting your dog run freely, always supervising your dog around children, and making sure that he is properly identified. Good manners mean that you set a high standard of dog ownership by never infringing on the rights of other people and dogs in public places. When traveling, make certain that your puppy doesn't bark if crated in a hotel room or relieve himself in inappropriate areas. At the dog park, if your dog is trying to play with another dog, and the other dog clearly is not interested, stop your dog from bothering the other dog. If your dog has the bad habit of jumping up when greeting people, you must stop him from doing so. If your dog goes to the bathroom in a public place, clean it up; walking away and pretending that you don't see it only increases anti-dog sentiment, which is why dogs aren't allowed many places. Finally, quality of life means attention to your dog's training and overall care.

There's time in every training regimen for plenty of puppy cuddles.

The other part of the test assesses certain areas of your puppy's temperament as well as his competency in learned behaviors. For example, the evaluator will watch for any signs of aggression toward people and other puppies throughout the training course. At the conclusion of the course, your puppy will be tested on "pre-CGC" behaviors, including accepting petting from someone other than you, tolerating handling of his ears and feet, walking on a leash past other people from about 5 feet away, and performing the *sit, down, stay,* and *come* exercises. He will also be presented with distractions, and his reactions are gauged. The supervised separation, in which you leave your puppy with another person while you walk 10 feet away, is important for your dog's confidence level and is tested further in the Canine Good Citizen test.

In addition to the satisfaction of having completed the AKC S.T.A.R. Puppy Program successfully with your puppy, your puppy will receive a medal and certificate, you'll receive a handbook and monthly newsletter from the AKC, and you'll be eligible for a discount on the AKC Companion Animal Recovery (AKC CAR) service.

Public Manners

Of course, you have the most adorable puppy in the world, but not everyone loves dogs, and not everyone who loves dogs will necessarily love your dog. Dog lovers should stick together, so you should become a good ambassador for other dog owners when you and

CANINE GOOD CITIZEN

The AKC's Canine Good Citizen® (CGC) Program is designed to reward dogs who have good manners at home and in the community. A two-part program that stresses responsible pet ownership for owners and basic good manners for dogs, the CGC Program lays the best foundation for training for various AKC activities such as rally, obedience, tracking, and agility.

You can attend a basic training or CGC class to teach your dog the CGC behaviors, or, if you have the skills and knowledge, you can teach your dog the CGC skills yourself. When your dog is ready, you'll sign up for a CGC test administered by an AKC-approved CGC Evaluator. Tests are held at dog shows, at some training classes, and at a number of pet superstores, and some evaluators make appointments to test dogs. When your dog passes the CGC test, the evaluator will give you the paperwork to send to the AKC to request the CGC certificate. To find an evaluator near you, visit www.akc.org/events/cgc/cgc_bystate.cfm.

In a little over one decade, the Canine Good Citizen Program has begun to have an extremely positive impact on many of our communities, and various nations around the world have modeled their own tests after the AKC template. In order to receive the CGC certificate, a dog must pass the ten-step test that includes the following skills, all of which are done on leash:

Test 1: Accepting a friendly stranger—The dog will allow a friendly stranger to approach him and speak to the handler in a natural, everyday situation.

Test 2: Sitting politely for petting—The dog will allow a friendly stranger to pet him while he is out with his handler.

Test 3: Appearance and grooming—The dog will welcome being groomed and examined and will permit someone, such as a veterinarian, groomer, or friend of the owner, to do so.

Test 4: Out for a walk (walking on a loose lead)—The handler/dog team will take a short "walk" to show that the dog is under control while walking on leash.

Test 5: Walking through a crowd—The dog and handler walk around and pass close to several people (at least three) to demonstrate that the dog can move about politely in pedestrian traffic and is under control in public places.

Test 6: Sit and down on command and staying in place—The dog will respond to the handler's commands to *sit* and *down* and will remain in the place when commanded by the handler (*sit* or *down* position, whichever the handler prefers).

Test 7: Coming when called—The dog will come when called by the handler. The handler will walk 10 feet away from the dog, turn to face the dog, and call the dog.

Test 8: Reaction to another dog—To demonstrate that the dog can behave politely around other dogs, two handlers and their dogs approach each other from a distance of about 20 feet, stop, shake hands and exchange pleasantries, and continue on for about 10 feet.

Test 9: Reaction to distraction—To demonstrate the dog is confident when faced with common distracting situations, the evaluator will select and present two distractions. Examples of distractions include dropping a chair, rolling a crate dolly past the dog, having a jogger run in front of the dog, and dropping a crutch or cane.

Test 10: Supervised separation—This test demonstrates that a dog can be left with a trusted person, if necessary, and will maintain training and good manners. Evaluators are encouraged to say something like, "Would you like me to watch your dog?" and then take hold of the dog's leash. The owner will go out of sight for three minutes.

To learn more about the CGC test and for detailed instructions on training for the ten skills required for a well-mannered dog, consult Dr. Mary Burch's award-winning book *Citizen Canine*, available in paperbook or e-book.

A well-socialized dog is prepared to accept attention from strangers.

your puppy are around other people. Do not allow your puppy to jump up on anyone, paw at anyone, or nudge anyone with his muzzle when he wants to be petted. Your dog should be in a *sit/stay* position when meeting another person, and allow the person to decide if he or she wants to interact with your dog.

You also must remember that not every dog wants to meet and play with your puppy—even if he is the cutest puppy in the world—so do not allow your puppy to run up to strange dogs. If your puppy is interested in meeting another dog, ask the dog's owner politely and respectfully if your dog can approach and say hello. Do not expect every dog to want to be approached by your dog. If another dog initiates the contact and your puppy is interested, be sure that you and the other dog's owner supervise their interactions.

The best way to ensure that your puppy becomes a well-behaved member of society is to take him through the AKC's Canine Good Citizen® Program. A Canine Good Citizen is a dog who will be welcome in any dog-friendly home (after all, who wants friends who don't like dogs?) and will be a polite member of society when you're out in public, around strangers, and around other dogs.

VACATIONING WITH YOUR DOG

Sunny beaches, spacious campgrounds, national and state parks, quaint historical towns—there are so many possibilities for vacationing with your dog. There are bed-and-breakfasts with amenities designed with the comfort of four-legged guests in mind. Some pet-friendly accommodations have staff members who will take your dog for potty walks while you are out and about, while others offer organized activities, such as hikes, for dogs and their owners. Outdoor enthusiasts can enjoy weekend-long camps for dogs and their owners that include hiking, swimming, and educational courses on topics such as pet first aid, canine massage, training, and grooming.

When vacationing with your dog, remember that not everyone loves dogs, so do your part to keep the "nay-dog-sayers" at bay. Bring enough clean-up bags so that you can always pick up after your dog. In hotels, make sure that your dog is quiet, and don't allow him up on the bed or other furniture where he will leave hair behind. Pet-friendly hotels are difficult enough to find, so be responsible and don't let your dog be the one who ruins it for other dogs and their owners.

The best way to prepare for the AKC CGC test is to attend a solid obedience course that teaches the exercises necessary for the test. You can then reinforce what you learn in class each week by practicing your dog's obedience skills in an area with distractions, such as strangers and other dogs, present.

There are several advantages to your dog's earning the CGC title. One is that many homeowners' insurance companies will offer you a discount on your policy. Some companies that would normally not insure you may consider insuring you if you show proof that your dog has earned the CGC award. The CGC award is also an excellent foundation for therapy dog training.

Welcoming Guests to Your Home

Before you invite your favorite aunt ("the cat lady") to your home or host a dinner party for your spouse's boss, make sure that you have control over your canine toddler. If your puppy goes crazy with excitement every time the doorbell rings, you have some real training to do before exposing your guests to your pup.

Before you open your front door—every time—place your puppy in a *sit/stay* position and do not allow him to get up until you release him. Your guests should be told, "Please do not pet my dog; he's in training," which people will understand and appreciate. It is only after the person has entered the house and your dog has remained in a nice, steady *sit/stay* that you should release him from the position. If people want to pet the dog, allow them to do so only after you've released him from the *sit/stay*. Keep in mind that petting is a form of praise, so being petted by you or your guests is an appropriate reward for the puppy's holding the *sit/stay* and getting up only when you told him to.

Guests do not always close doors behind them, and puppies don't know that dashing out the front door may lead them into danger. Many dogs have been lost or hurt this way. Keep your puppy's leash on or keep him on a house line when you are expecting visitors.

If you have a landscaper or if other people, such as meter readers or pool cleaners, enter your yard, make sure that your puppy does not go out into the yard until you've checked that all gates have been securely closed. A gate could be left open, allowing the dog to escape.

1. In this S.T.A.R. Puppy class, puppies were often accompanied by more than one of their owners.

2. Six-month-old German Shorthaired Pointer Bella proudly shows off her AKC S.T.A.R. Puppy medal.

3. Five-month-old Nitro's Freedom Liberty Belle with her S.T.A.R. Puppy accolades. "Liberty" is the granddaughter of the 2009 AKC Award for Canine Excellence (ACE) in Law Enforcement winner, Am./Can. Ch. Nitro's' Boy Wonder ("Robin").

4. S.T.A.R. Puppy grads and their proud owners pose on the agility course.

5. CGC evaluator Mary Anne Coleman with her Border Collie, Nike, a S.T.A.R. Puppy graduate.

CHAPTER 7

Common Puppy Problems

Puppies will be puppies, just as kids will be kids! Most puppy "problem behaviors" are natural to dogs and are only "problems" to us humans. Puppies are just doing what puppies do and are simply learning to understand what's expected of them in a human world.

A puppy does what he wants to do because it feels good to him. There is a payoff: he receives some sort of satisfaction from his actions. He doesn't understand that his owners perceive many self-rewarding puppy behaviors as "unwanted." Owners must set ground rules right from the start and teach the puppy that unwanted behavior has consequences. If you ignore unwanted behavior, it doesn't go away; rather, it will only get worse or, at the very least, will always be present on some level. For example, a puppy that is never taught proper bite inhibition may not always nip, but he will eventually evolve into a very mouthy dog. He will grab at your arms, legs, shirt, or whatever else he can get his mouth

on when he wants your attention because he was never taught that this behavior is unwelcome.

Quite often, a puppy's owners do not correct unwanted behavior because they are not sure how to, and they may think that their corrections will do more harm than good. Trainers agree that if you give your dog a correction, and the correction doesn't lead to any signs of stopping the behavior, then what you think of as a correction may not be perceived as such to the dog. You must communicate with your puppy in a way that he understands. For example, if you say to a child, "*Ne courez pas dans la rue*," and the child doesn't speak French, he or she will not understand that you said, "Do not run into the street," and the child will go ahead and run into the street.

Nipping and Mouthing

It would seem that a puppy's brain is in his mouth, as his whole world seems to revolve around it. Your puppy spends the first eight or more weeks of his life mouthing on his littermates in play, so when he comes home with you, it is quite normal for him to want to constantly put his mouth on whatever he can. Dogs feel things with their mouths. They do not have the same type of tactile stimulation with their paws as we do with our hands. Puppies usually engage in mouthy behavior until they are around five months old. Pups use their mouths to investigate everything, which can include your arms and hands, if you don't do something to stop it. Nipping hurts quite a bit, as those tiny puppy teeth are sharp.

The puppy's mother likely growled or barked at her litter when one of the pups bit too hard. A new owner can communicate the same way with his or her new puppy, and the pup will understand. Give your puppy a sharp and startling "Ouch!" (or a similar noise)

Until you teach him otherwise, your puppy will consider your fingers quite chew-worthy.

Improper mouthing is a behavior that needs to be "nipped" in the bud.

every time he nips you. It's not necessary to use the word "no" every time the puppy does something that's unwanted. Trainers who overuse "no" render the word virtually meaningless to the puppy, who begins to think that it's the only word his owner knows (or that it must be his name!). If you are consistent with discouraging nipping, you will soon see a difference in the puppy's behavior. At first, the pup may seem startled or uncertain, but you should be able to resolve the issue in three to five days.

Whining and Barking

Barking is a lot easier to correct than whining. Dogs usually whine because they want something: a walk, food, water, a toy, or play. You may think whining is annoying, but keep in mind that whining is one way a puppy communicates. If he's whining for water (because his bowl is empty), you need to give him water. If you find that he is whining incessantly, and you cannot determine what he's trying to tell you, engage the puppy in an activity or a quick two-minute training session. Redirecting his attention onto you and something positive shows him that you're the one who makes decisions and that he should rely on you for whatever he needs.

A puppy may bark at what he sees on the other side of the fence.

Fortunately, most dogs will bark rather than whine. It is important to discourage excessive barking right away. Barking, of course, can be purposeful in dogs, and it's their primary means of vocal expression. Dogs will bark because they are protecting their territory, alerting their owners to the presence of someone or something, or issuing a warning of some kind. If you know why your puppy is barking, he will stop barking when you handle the issue he's "telling" you about—for instance, that there's someone at the door or that a person is walking his or her dog in front of your house (without your permission—in the puppy's mind!). Tell the puppy, "I got this" or "It's OK" and he will settle down.

If the puppy is barking needlessly and excessively, then you have an actual concern. Many dogs bark because it's fun—it's a self-gratifying activity. The worst thing you can do is bark back at him with "No, no, no! Stop that!" The puppy will think you agree with him, and his barking will raise the roof.

To dissuade your puppy from barking, you will need a treat and a squeaky toy, along with a clicker (if you're using one). When the puppy is quiet, give him a treat (or click and treat) for good behavior. Once he starts to bark, squeak the toy to distract him, and when he responds to the squeaking and looks for the toy, give him a treat (or click and treat). Practice this lesson a few times a day and be patient.

The key to solving any behavior problem is understanding the function of the behavior. For example, a dog may bark because there is a squirrel in the yard, a herding dog might bark if something is moving, or dogs left in an apartment all day while their owner works may bark because they are simply bored. The first and easiest preventive measure is to provide the dog with an activity that he can do in place of barking—such as an interactive toy that is stuffed with peanut butter or has treats hidden inside.

Make sure before you leave home (if that is when the barking happens) that you give your pup some rigorous exercise—this will increase the likelihood that he'll be more relaxed and may even take a nap.

For the hard-core, excessive barker for whom all the standard tips don't seem to work, an experienced trainer, such as an AKC S.T.A.R. Puppy trainer or an animal behaviorist, can work with you to solve the problem. Animal behaviorists will be able to do a functional analysis to determine the situations under which barking occurs. If the barking means that you could lose your condo and you and your dog could end up on the street, you can consider using a humane no-bark device such as a citronella collar while you're working to address the problem.

Jumping Up

Puppies jump. They jump because they jumped on their littermates, and they jump because they get satisfaction from it. Jumping up brings your puppy closer to your face, and the face is a primary contact point for puppies within a pack. If your puppy jumps up on you and you push him back onto the floor, he will jump up again to seek your attention. Owners unknowingly reinforce this unwanted behavior the first day their cute bouncy puppies come home. Each and every time you put your hands on your vertical, attention-seeking puppy, you are actually rewarding him for jumping up. Remember, hands-on attention is praise to your puppy.

No matter how small the puppy or how innocuous the behavior may seem, jumping is not a habit that you should encourage.

Even if you don't usually mind your puppy's jumping up, your puppy won't be able to tell when it's OK for him to jump up and when it's not OK. He will not understand that you have your favorite work dress on or that you'd rather not have muddy footprints on your clothes after he's come inside from the yard on a rainy day. He will also not understand that it is dangerous to jump up on your pregnant neighbor or your three-year-old nephew. The best thing to do is teach your puppy to never jump up.

The best way to discourage your puppy from jumping up is to ignore the behavior, both physically and verbally. That means you don't push the puppy down, and you don't say "No, no, get off me!"—both of these actions have won the puppy the attention he was seeking. When the puppy jumps up on you, immediately turn around and step away from him (which is exactly what he doesn't want to happen). After attempting to jump up on you a few times, and each time getting no response, he may give up and keep his four paws on the floor.

If your dog is starved for attention, and this is fueling his constant jumping up, you may simply need to spend more time with him. Dogs who get plenty of exercise are usually easier to train. Likewise, you can redirect the dog's attention to a lesson, such as *sit* or *sit/stay*. Lavish him with hands-on praise when he performs the exercise, thereby reinforcing in the dog that there are positive ways to get attention, which are always more effective than jumping up.

Many trainers use the *off* command to stop unwanted jumping behavior. The dog may be jumping up on you, a visitor, the couch, or the kitchen counter. Say "Off" in a tone that gets the dog's attention and point and look toward the floor.

Chewing

If puppies' brains are in their mouths, then chewing is just thinking! Chewing, for the first few months, is most puppies' main occupation. Remember, they do not use their paws the way we use our hands; they use their mouths to learn about the world. Chewing also makes puppies' mouths feel better when they are teething.

The safest toys for your puppy are hard rubber toys, and he will especially enjoy those that can be filled with food treats. Peanut butter works very well, as it is a great source of protein, and your puppy has to work hard to get the peanut butter out of the toy. Another nutritious idea is to smash a banana into the toy and freeze it. The cold feels great on the puppy's gums, and the banana is loaded with potassium, which is good for a growing puppy.

If you fall down on the job and fail to supervise your puppy at all times while he's free in the house, and you find him chewing on a forbidden object, distract him by clapping your hands loudly and immediately take the object away from him. After a few moments, give him a safe chew toy. As long as you're consistent and persistent, he will eventually learn that there are appropriate and inappropriate things to chew.

A teething puppy will try to get his mouth on whatever he can.

Begging

Begging at the table, for dogs or humans, is not good manners. It is, in fact, one of the easiest problems to prevent. Simply put, do not feed your dog any food from the table—*ever*. Teach your dog to lie down during dinner in his designated spot. If he gets up and approaches the table, distract the puppy with a loud noise and tell him "Go to your place" or whatever cue you use to tell him to go to his special area.

Tell your guests not to feed your dog any scraps from the table. When you're in the kitchen preparing food, make sure not to toss your dog any tidbits from the counter.

If it's too late, and you've succumbed to sharing your steak (and chicken cutlets and fish sticks and spaghetti) with your pup, you likely have a seasoned beggar who whimpers, paws, and barks for his fair share at suppertime. An easy solution to the problem is simply to put your puppy in his crate before you sit down to eat. Be sure to give the puppy something to play with in his crate. Once he starts to chew on his toy, give him praise and a treat and walk away.

An active puppy will be happier and calmer if he gets adequate training and plenty of exercise.

Even with a talented beggar, the "Go to your place" solution is the best, though you may have to practice this lesson throughout the day (not during mealtimes) and work up to commanding the dog while you're actually sitting at the kitchen table. Each time he goes to his spot, praise him, pet him, and give him a treat. Extend the amount of time that the puppy spends in his spot each day, and do not let the puppy get up without your release word. Don't give up, or you'll never be able to enforce this exercise once the sweet smell of fried chicken is in the air!

Excitability

"My dog is just crazy!" "I can't control my puppy unless he's sleeping." "My dog needs professional help." Excitability—complaints of an out-of-control dog—often incites owners to contact a professional trainer. More often than not, it's the owners' failure to train their dog that leads to the dog's becoming out of control. Once an owner starts a dedicated obedience-training regimen, most of your puppy's problem behaviors, including excitability, jumping up, nipping, and so forth, will begin to disappear.

Some dogs are very active by nature; others are more laid back. If you researched your chosen breed, then you should know the breed's temperament (and therefore what you're getting into) before you acquire a puppy. Sporting dogs, herding dogs, and terriers, for instance, are known for their high activity levels, while hounds tend to be calmer in general. As long as you channel your puppy's energy into positive activities to supplement obedience training, you will have a great companion.

Separation Issues

The diagnosis of "separation behavior" is often overused when evaluating dogs' problems. A dog who goes to the bathroom in the house when his owner is away or who barks or cries in his crate when left alone is not necessarily suffering from separation issues. A true separation issue is when a dog paces for hours, scratches and chews through a door to get through to the other side, injures himself trying to escape, and destroys household items. This kind of destruction does not refer to gnawing on a chair leg or stealing the meat you left to defrost in the sink; rather, it refers to escalated forms of destruction.

Solving a real separation-behavior problem is often a matter of obedience training and increasing your dog's exercise. You can help your dog cope with separation issues by following a habitual and expected routine. Begin a simple morning routine in which you leave the house in a low-key manner. Before you leave, take your dog for a nice long walk and throw a favorite toy around with him to help him expend some of his energy. Make sure that your house is at a comfortable temperature. Trainers commonly recommend

A puppy with no suitable outlets for his energy can turn to all sorts of destructive behavior.

leaving the television or stereo on so the puppy does not feel alone; the sounds of human voices will comfort him while you are not home. Right before you leave, put your puppy in his crate with his favorite toy. Make it a simple departure and a low-key goodbye; do not fuss over him. If he starts crying or whimpering as you leave the house, do not go back inside to try to console him.

You set your dog up for misbehavior when you leave tempting treats within his reach.

Shyness

Not everyone has a "so-excited-to-meet-you" dog, and not everyone wants one, either. Some dogs tend to be shier and more reserved than others. If you have a dog who tends to be on the shy side, the best thing to do is take him out as often as possible to dog-friendly places where he will have the opportunity to meet a lot of new faces.

If possible, sit outside at a coffee shop with your dog. Coffee shops usually have a high volume of customers, so there will be a constant stream of people coming and going, many of whom will want to pet your puppy. When they ask, allow them to reach down and greet your puppy. Do not let your puppy hide behind you and do not console your puppy if he shows signs of fear; in fact, do just the opposite, as consoling him will simply reinforce his fear. Your goal is to desensitize him to strangers so that he feels more comfortable around people. You will find that the more often you don't coddle him and you allow people to pet him, the sooner you will build your puppy's confidence and teach him to calm himself when he's feeling stressed.

Counter Surfing

Counter surfing is a hobby for the hungry hound! Like begging, counter surfing is a very self-rewarding activity. Your puppy should not have access to the kitchen without your supervision, so counter surfing should never become an issue. There are too many things in the kitchen that a puppy can get into, some of which—such as chocolate candy, nuts, grapes, raisins, and other common foods—are dangerous to him. At the very least, allowing him free run of the kitchen can cause him to develop some bad habits. If you leave food on the counter, it's an invitation for your puppy to steal it and devour it before anyone catches him. If you're not home or you're in another room, you won't catch him in the act; plus, the reward is way too valuable for any consequence to have an effect.

Set the puppy up for success. If he is in the kitchen with you while you are preparing food, keep everything edible out of his reach. You can redirect the dog with a treat, though the dog may decide that he's succeeded in getting your attention and a treat, and thus he will feel rewarded for his behavior. Distracting him with a squeaky toy is often a successful method. Removing the rewards (food) from the countertops is the definitive way to end this unwanted behavior.

CHAPTER 8

Training and Communication

If you've gotten this far into the book, then you must agree that there are real benefits to training your dog, whether he's going to perform in the show ring, a competitive field, or just your backyard. When a dog is well behaved, the dog is happier, his owners are happier, and the household is harmonious and sane. Training stops a dog from destroying his owners' home and belongings, thus saving his owners a lot of frustration, heartbreak, and money. Training also saves dogs' lives; for example, trained dogs are less likely to run out into traffic or get into other dangerous situations because they listen to their owners' commands.

Trained dogs are happier emotionally, physically, and psychologically. When a dog is trained, he has jobs to do to keep him occupied and draw worth from, whether sitting and staying while pizza is being delivered or lying down in his special area during the family's dinnertime or standing still on the veterinarian's exam table for his checkup. No job is too small

No matter the type of training, the key to success is communicating with your dog.

for your dog—he wants to please you. Proficiency in basic skills also opens up doors for dogs to participate with their owners in therapy work or compete in organized sports, including obedience, conformation, rally, agility, and breed-specific events such as herding trials or field trials.

Obedience training sets the groundwork for the rules by which we want our dogs to live. We humans can be a bit selfish, and we feel that our lives would be infinitely better if our dogs simply did what we asked them to do when we asked them to do it. Dogs do not fare well as their own leaders in the human world, so you have to become your puppy's leader. Have you ever had a boss who really didn't know how to do his or her job properly? If you let your dog take charge, it will create a similar situation—you will have a leader who doesn't make the best decisions. It is amazing that the typical problems people have with their dogs—jumping, digging, chewing, barking, and so forth—actually cease to exist with some good obedience training. When you teach a dog to substitute an acceptable behavior in place of an unacceptable behavior, you are giving him something purposeful to do, thus stimulating him mentally, physically, and psychologically. You are making him a balanced, well-behaved dog with a job, and he is happier and more secure because you are happy with him. Obedience training gives you the tools to teach your dog what to do and what not to do so that you can stop him from engaging in undesirable behavior and encourage him to do the right thing instead.

Training isn't just about discouraging unwelcome behavior; it's about ingraining good manners into your daily routine with your dog. For example, when you are going to take your dog outside, teach him to do a *sit/stay* as you put the leash on him before you walk out the door. Isn't that easier than trying to catch him?

When you are walking down the street with your dog, isn't it wonderful to know that despite the neighbor's aggressive dog barking and lunging at him as you pass, your dog will continue walking and will seem not to notice that the other dog is there? Isn't this preferable to being dragged across the street by your dog so he can bark back?

A trained dog is also a pleasure to take to the dog park. When it is time to go home, all you have to do is call your dog, and he will come running to sit politely in front of you while you put his leash on and praise him for being such a good listener. You won't have to chase him or call him over and over.

A puppy responds positively to affection and his owner's upbeat attitude.

Dog Spoken Here

Who are we humans to preach about communication? Humans communicate through an estimated 6,500 spoken languages and 200 sign languages, while dogs basically speak one. We humans have so much to learn from the animal kingdom, and there are so many ways that animals communicate with each other and with us. There are also many signs and signals that humans give their dogs without even realizing it. Dogs read our smells, our eyes, our body language, and our voices, and they respond to our energy and moods, positive or negative, high or low.

Owners quite often become frustrated with their dogs' behavior, thinking that dogs have the capacity to reason, respond, and react in the same way that humans do, which of

---

BODY LANGUAGE

Dogs are more sensitive to body language than humans and thus are more responsive to it as well. They learn what humans want by watching their owners' body language; dogs do not understand all of the verbal language we use, but they can determine a lot about a person's energy and actions and the environment around them just by visual observation. Dogs also use body language to communicate with each other, with people, and with other animals.

Play behavior: Puppies just want to have fun. Running up to you and barking, backing up with his tail wagging, barking at you again, running up to you again—this is a typical puppy scenario and shows that your puppy wants to play and is trying to get you to chase him. When your puppy conveys that he wants to have some fun, seize the opportunity! You can turn playtime into a thinking game by moving from side to side, teasing your puppy just a bit, and making it a challenge for him to figure out in which direction you're going to go next. Hide a toy behind your back to pique his curiosity and encourage him to run around behind you to find it. Use your puppy's play behavior as an opportunity to bond with him.

Biting and growling: An owner often panics when the new puppy runs up, bites him or her hard, and then backs up and growls. The owner may think that the new puppy is vicious, but it is really just the puppy's way of trying out his voice, learning about the world, and discovering the consequences of his actions. Nevertheless, puppies have razor-sharp teeth and must be taught proper bite inhibition. You must enforce a zero-tolerance policy on biting.

Submissive urination: This can be common in young puppies, whose bladder control is not yet fully developed. If a puppy gets excited or thinks that he is about to be corrected for an undesirable behavior, he will squat and urinate. If this becomes an issue when people approach your puppy, the best thing to do is move your puppy away so that he doesn't feel as if his space is being invaded. Let the puppy approach the strangers on his own time, when he feels ready.

course they do not. So if other thinking, rational humans don't always behave the way we want them to, how can we expect good behavior all the time from our dogs?

If we want our dogs to become balanced, happy beings, we must give them all of the information they need to understand what we are trying to tell them. We must praise our dogs for jobs well done. If we want them to learn something, we must guide them in the right direction and help them make the right decisions. We also need to give our dogs opportunities to make choices on their own, and we need to correct them for any wrong decisions that they make.

There is no place for anger in training—that means no yelling, no hitting, no screaming, and no grabbing the puppy by the scruff of his neck. Once you get to the point of

Fear behavior: You know your puppy is in fear mode when you see some or all of these body-language signs: cowering, a stiff body, the tail tucked down, the ears held back, a low growl, an arched back, or an intense gaze. Your instinct is often to soothe your dog; however, when your puppy is not sure of himself, he needs to learn to self-soothe. If you console your puppy each time he shows fear, he won't learn to deal with stressful circumstances and build up a tolerance for stress. If your puppy frequently displays fear behavior, you should consult a professional trainer for guidance, as this is not something that a puppy will simply "grow out of." Fear will get worse over time if it is not addressed and resolved.

Potty signs: Clearly, when your puppy starts furiously sniffing and going around in circles, he is about to go potty, and this is behavior that you want to look out for. If you see your puppy about to relieve himself in the house, you can pick him up and bring him outside. If you catch the puppy squatting or in the middle of having an accident, make a big noise as you scoop him up and quickly bring him outside; this should make him tense up so that he stops what he's doing and finishes once you put him down in the proper spot outdoors.

Wagging tail: The mistaken notion that a wagging tail always means that a dog is happy and friendly is very common. There are, of course, happy wagging tails—think of a Golden Retriever enthusiastically returning to his owner with a fetched ball. Then, there are stiffly wagging tails, either held very high or hanging down, slowly moving back and forth. If you see a dog whose tail is moving stiffly and slowly, do not assume that he is being friendly. If you see a dog who is tense and leaning slightly forward, almost on his tiptoes, with a wagging tail, this is not a good sign, either. A dog in this position is being very cautious, and if something startles him or he detects a scent he doesn't like, he could suddenly bark at, snap at, or even bite your dog.

Watch your puppy and, most importantly, watch other dogs' reactions to your puppy. Not all dogs will have the same sweet, tender personality that your puppy has, and you want to protect your puppy. The more you watch the body language of other dogs, the better you will become at reading your own dog's body language, which will make you a better owner.

Choosing a canine companion whose energy level matches your own is a great start to a rewarding relationship.

anger, you are out of control, and if you cannot control your own actions, you certainly are not going to be able to control your dog's actions. When you find yourself angry, frustrated, or very emotional, take a breath and walk away. Stay calm and carry on.

When we issue verbal cues, dogs respond to our tone, our pitch, the sound of the words, our body language, and the situation, all at the same time. They are much more in tune with our body language than we are with theirs. Try issuing your cues in different tones of voice to see how the results change. For example, if you say "Remy, DOWN" very loudly, he will not respond as well as he will when you issue the cue in a voice that's just above a whisper. The *down* position is a relaxing one. Who can lie down and relax if someone is shouting "Lie down!" in a harsh voice? Think of putting a baby to bed. You softly rock the baby and talk in a soothing voice before putting him or her in the crib.

A similar example is when you call your dog to come to you. Think of how you would react if your significant other came home and called out in a happy, upbeat tone, "Honey, I'm home! Come here so I can show you something!" You would probably run to the front door in anticipation. But if he or she walked in the door and said abruptly, "Get over here now," you would probably keep doing whatever you were doing, pretending not to hear. It's the same thing with your dog. Any cue that requires action, such as *come* or *heel*, needs to be given in a positive, encouraging tone of voice. Anything that requires a *stay* after it, such as *sit* or *down*, needs a quiet but direct tone.

An excellent exercise to do with your dog is to take five minutes each day and communicate with him using only your body. For example, if you want your puppy to come to you, crouch down and encourage him toward you by clapping your hands. Have him walk with you. Place him into a *sit/stay*. Send him to his bed. Make him stand for examination. Whatever you do, do not use your voice. This will force you to see how much you can get your dog to do just through body language.

Once you have issued cues with your entire body, spend a few minutes communicating using just your face. Watch how your puppy responds when you smile, squint, look at him sternly, and laugh with glee at his doing something the right way. This will help you realize how much communication is actually silent, and how much your dog responds to your body language.

You will want to do these exercises three times a week for a couple of weeks; you can even do them when you are training with a clicker. This learning experience is not so much for your puppy as it is for you.

Before you can attempt to teach your puppy anything, he must be paying attention to you.

Think Positive!

Take a few minutes each day before training to visualize a perfect scenario with your dog. You will be much more relaxed, you'll have positive energy, and your training sessions will be more productive.

1. Sit and imagine what the perfect dog is to you. Is he visiting people in a nursing home? Is he reading with schoolchildren? Is he entertaining people by performing tricks?
2. Close your eyes and spend three minutes or so visualizing your relationship with your dog and walking yourself through the scenario, with your dog doing everything that you want him to do.

Along with your visualizations, take time to create some positive affirmations. Before you start each session, make a list of what you want to address with your dog. Does he need more practice walking on leash? Do you want to build up to a three-minute *sit/stay*? Are you still having trouble walking him past the house down the street with the distracting, barking dog? Once you have determined your objectives, write out the goals in positive statements:

1. Today, Sammy will walk perfectly past the pigeons.
2. Today, Sammy will do a one-minute *sit/stay* in front of the coffee shop
3. Today, Sammy will ignore the neighbor's dog.

Stay away from statements such as "I want" and "I hope." Word your statements as though they will actually happen. For example, instead of "I don't want Sammy to run after little Johnny on his bicycle," you should write "Sammy is going to ignore little Johnny on his bicycle."

Don't give up on a stubborn puppy. Keep practicing and thinking positive until he's following your cues.

Practicing On Your Own

Many times, despite being relaxed and positive for your training sessions, you will still have trouble teaching your puppy his lessons. A terrific exercise is to practice without the dog before you try to teach him something new. Remember, Ginger Rogers did everything that Fred Astaire did, but backward and in high heels. You must master the moves yourself before trying to coordinate them with a partner.

For example, if you are having trouble with heeling, keep little Sassy in her crate while you practice first without her. Do your breathing and visualization exercises, then start walking, keeping your arm down and relaxed, as you go through the steps of having your puppy walk on leash. Say "Let's walk," use your hand signals, and pretend to put your pup in a *sit/stay* at the end of the exercise. Be sure to give your pretend puppy a lot of praise.

To practice the *come* exercise by yourself, stand up tall and breathe slowly and regularly. Put your left arm out to the side and bring your left hand to your right shoulder. In your happiest voice, say "Come! Good dog, come!" If you practice this a few times without the puppy, you'll become comfortable with the tone of your voice and with your body language. These two things are very important, as you want to use a cheerful voice and welcoming body language, such as crouching down and clapping your hands in encouragement.

The *heel* and *come* are just two examples of the foundation behaviors that can be tricky when you first try them with your dog. By practicing them first without your dog, you will be more at ease with how to properly teach the skills, and your puppy will learn more quickly.

Clicker Training

A lesson borrowed from the world of marine mammals, clicker training is now also a very popular method of training dogs and cats. The clicker, which is a small handheld tool that makes a clicking noise when pressed, is a great tool for getting a puppy's attention, marking good behavior, and teaching your puppy to focus on you. The clicker allows you to reward your puppy from a distance, and it helps you become more adept at timing your rewards and watching your dog's body language.

Treats are used as rewards in clicker training, and the clicker allows you to let the dog know that the treat is coming. Some puppies become so distracted in the presence of treats that they cannot concentrate because they are so fixated on the food. This is how the clicker becomes an important tool, by serving as a "bridge" to the reward. The clicking sound lets the dog know that he has performed the desired behavior and that a treat is soon to be delivered. The clicking sound does not replace the treat; rather, it enhances the reward by creating motivation without the distraction of food.

You can easily teach your puppy to associate treats and praise with a clicker in a short period of time. Freeze-dried liver broken into tiny pieces are ideal treats. Remember, the bigger the treats, the more your puppy will have to chew, and the less immediate and effective your reward will be. Larger treats will also fill up your puppy faster, making him less responsive to the treats; as a result, training will be less productive.

In your first clicker session, sit with your puppy indoors and have some treats near you where he cannot find them. Let your puppy do his thing, and as he moves away from you, click the clicker. When he responds to the sound, give him a treat. Let him sniff and play, and then click again; when he comes to you, give him a treat. Do this for about five minutes to teach the puppy that when he hears the click, coming to you will result in a treat for him.

The next day, move your training into another room and do the same thing you did on the first day. Make sure that you pay attention to your puppy's every move; this second day is more about practice for you than it is for him. While you are reinforcing what your puppy is learning, you are also working on improving the timing of your rewards as well as your basic clicker-training skills (holding the treats, clicking the clicker, and watching your dog). Practice for ten minutes this time.

On day three, move to another safe, confined area, this time with some distractions. Practice for fifteen minutes, repeating what you've been doing for the last two days.

Once your puppy is making the connection between the clicker and the treats, you can start using the clicker with basic commands. In your next practice session, give your puppy the *sit* cue. Wait for your puppy to sit on his own and, once he does, click and treat. If the puppy doesn't respond to your cue immediately, hold the treat over his head until he sits, clicking and treating once he does. Become proficient with one cue before you move on to another. For example, work on the *sit* and then progress to the *stay*. Start to practice both and increase your puppy's repertoire by adding yet another cue.

Many trainers use clicker training solely to teach basic cues; however, you can use it for more advanced training once the basics are learned. For example, the clicker can be very helpful when you want to teach your puppy tricks, such as how to roll over or shake hands. Keep clickers handy—in your desk, in the kitchen, in the car. They are great fun and expand your skills as a trainer.

The initial goal of clicker training is to get your puppy's attention when he hears the click.

Changes during the First Year of Life

As your puppy matures, good manners may seem to become a thing of the past. This stage can begin as early as five to six months of age and as late as nine months of age. Your puppy is using less energy than he did as a puppy, but he's also bigger and stronger and can do a lot more damage. You may not be going to weekly training classes anymore, and your puppy is becoming more mature and more bold, resulting in a more determined and independent little creature.

Puppies will do things that drive you crazy. You may see your puppy reverting to mouthing, chewing, and other destructive behavior, leaving you to wonder if all of that training you did is just in your imagination.

There are a few things you can do to combat this "rebellious" stage; for example,

From newborn to adult in a relatively short time, a puppy experiences many physical and emotional changes during his first year of life.

change up your routine. Take a new route to the park so that your puppy can see different sights, smell new smells, and maybe even meet new people and dogs along the way. Start playing new games and finding different ways to exercise so that you keep your puppy challenged both mentally and physically. You might take him to an agility class or start a new hobby by preparing for therapy dog work. If you don't want to enroll in classes, you can start teaching your puppy tricks at home. There are useful tricks, such as teaching your pup to find and retrieve your keys, and classic tricks, such as teaching him to "speak" or "roll over and play dead" for entertainment.

Your adolescent puppy may start displaying behaviors such as food guarding, possessiveness, territory marking, and mounting. It is important when your puppy first comes home to work with him on allowing you to get near him while he is eating, playing, and sleeping. Some dogs protect their food, food dishes, toys, beds, or places on the furniture and, if approached, will growl, snap, threaten to bite, or bite. Animal behaviorists refer to this as *resource guarding.*

To teach your puppy not to guard his possessions, start early with touching his toys and dishes and letting him know that it is OK for you to do this. If your young puppy becomes tense or growls when you get too close to his food or a prized toy or "his" spot

Your adolescent dog may revert to more puppyish behavior, such as chewing on forbidden items.

on the couch, then you already have a resource guarder, and you need an organized plan.

First, start teaching your pup skills that can be used to manage his behavior such as *come*, *sit*, and *wait*. Next, throughout the day, work on the important skill of having your puppy give items, such as his squeaky toy or chew bone, to you when you say "Give." When he gives it to you, praise him, give him a treat, and then return the item to him so that he learns it is not the end of the world when you take something from him.

Resource guarding can be a serious behavior problem. If your puppy's resource guarding is bad enough that you could receive a serious bite or he could attack you, contact an animal behaviorist for help. If you have an older, larger puppy who is threatening to bite when you touch his food dish, stop feeding him from his bowl until you get the problem under control. Measure out the food he needs for his meals and use the food as rewards in short training sessions on *come*, *sit*, and *stay*. Some dogs, particularly dogs who have been in shelters or have had to compete with another dog for food, will guard their dishes. If you have multiple dogs in your household, and food guarding is a problem, start feeding your dogs with some space between them in or separate areas. Throughout the day, as your puppy complies with what you want him to do, be sure to reward him with treats, praise, or petting. The goal is to teach your puppy that good things come his way when he shows you good behavior.

Marking and mounting are common and natural behaviors for dogs, especially in their adolescence. Marking will certainly occur more frequently with a sexually intact dog of either sex; however, both spayed females and neutered males have been known to mark. There is nothing wrong with a dog marking outside, but it's an obvious problem indoors.

The best way to make progress in training? Together!

Mounting is a display of dominance, and it is important that a dog be stopped immediately each and every time he tries to mount a person. Dogs do not know that mounting humans is inappropriate and socially unacceptable, so it's up to us to tell them. As with marking, and all of the behaviors that can surface during adolescence, maintaining strong boundaries and giving your dog enough exercise should keep the potential for behavior problems during the teenage stage very low.

DOGS' SENSES

Puppies, just like humans, communicate using the five senses. They use their senses of smell and taste first (the vomeronasal organ in the roof of the mouth allows a dog to taste certain smells), followed by their sight, hearing, and touch. Knowing how dogs use their senses will help you understand your puppy more, and the more senses you use when training, the better. When a reward appeals to your dog's different senses, the results are quicker and the training is a lot more fun for both you and your dog.

SMELL

A canine's sense of smell is probably the most complex and most fascinating, yet the least understood, of the five senses. It is estimated that a dog's sense of smell is a million times more efficient than that of humans. The olfactory area in a dog's brain is forty times the size of a human's. The moisture on a dog's nose interacts with the molecules in the air, and the information is transmitted to the nerve impulses in the nose and then to the olfactory center in the brain. This is closely tied to the limbic system of the brain, which controls emotional responses.

Dogs mark with their scent for many reasons, such as designating their territory, whether in the wild or in the neighborhood. The family pet will mark the tree in front of his house so that other dogs know that the tree has been designated as "his" spot; it's a bit like leaving a calling card. When a dog smells the urine of another dog, he can determine the sex of the dog, whether the dog is sexually intact, and the direction in which the dog was traveling. A female's urine also tells other dogs whether she is in season. A dog doesn't just use his olfactory organs to figure out the world, they also help keep him cool.

TASTE

In so many ways, dogs' senses are far superior to ours, except when it comes to taste. Humans have the ability to recognize 9,000 different tastes, whereas dogs have the capacity to distinguish only about 2,000 tastes. Most of a dog's taste buds are densely packed around the tip of the tongue. When you give your dog a treat, the reward is both the taste of the food itself and the pleasurable feeling of the food going into the digestive tract.

Dogs use their sense of taste along with their sense of smell to gain information. When a dog sniffs something, he often will also lick it to learn more about the scent. Just behind a dog's front teeth is the vomeronasal organ, which is lined with olfactory receptor cells. If you see your dog licking the ground or another strange object, it means that he has picked up a scent on the object and wants to know more about it.

SIGHT

Newborn puppies are unable to see; by the fifteenth day, their eyes are usually open, but they still do not see very well until about the twenty-eighth day. It was thought at one time that dogs were unable to see in color, but it is now believed that they can see shades of black, gray, and blue.

Dogs do not see objects with as much definition as humans do, but their night vision is far superior to that of humans. A dog's eye is also much more sensitive to movement than the human's eye, so it is important to never make sudden movements toward a dog of any age.

When it comes to rewarding your dog, appealing to his sense of sight is very useful. When you are smiling, your dog will be happy and will know that he did something right. Even an older dog who doesn't hear very well understands the meaning of a human's smile and soft expression.

HEARING

The dog's sense of hearing is amazing; a puppy's hearing is fully developed by four weeks of age. Remember that humans use words, while dogs rely on pitch and volume, so it's important that the first sounds a puppy hears are not startling ones. A dog figures out a lot through sounds; for example, he learns that when he hears keys being picked up, it means his owner is leaving. A dog can also distinguish the sound, pitch, and rhythm of his owner's footsteps from those of others.

Dogs' sense of hearing is stronger than humans', and dogs are also able to listen to two sounds at one time, one in each ear. Dogs hear a range of sounds four times greater than humans do, which means that they can hear higher pitches than we can (e.g., the "dog whistle" that humans cannot hear) and sounds that are much farther away. If you think that your dog is barking or growling for no reason, he's likely reacting to something that you cannot hear.

Appeal to your dog's sense of hearing during training by using the volume and tone of your voice to gently encourage him, happily praise him, or firmly correct him.

TOUCH

We receive calming benefits from petting our dogs, and dogs receive similar benefits when touched by humans. When a dog undergoes stress, such as during a thunderstorm, it is normal for him to seek the comfort of his human family members. He might rest his head on his owner's leg or crawl up into his owner's lap. The touch of his owner and the closeness and social interaction that come with it are comforting to the dog.

It is important to remember, though, that if a dog was not socialized and did not experience being petted and handled as a puppy, he will be very sensitive to any type of touch from humans, whether you're putting his collar on him, clipping his nails, or rubbing his ears as a form of affection.

Dogs have sensory receptors on their faces, which is why socialized dogs love being pet on their faces and heads; it is a very comfortable feeling for them. It also explains how a newborn pup can find his mother's teats by just feeling around before he can hear or see.

Using touch to praise your dog is very effective and allows for an immediate response. For example, if you are guiding your dog gently into the *sit* position, your hands are already on him, so you are praising him as he is sitting; this makes sitting pleasurable to him.

Massage is a terrific way to bond with your dog; it can have a very soothing effect on your dog by increasing serotonin levels, and it can help you relax, too. Massage can also help touch-sensitive dogs become more tolerant of human touch.

CHAPTER 9

Obedience Skills

Obedience skills are important for many reasons. They not only boost a dog's confidence but they also give us, as owners, the tools to stop problem behaviors. For example, if your puppy tries to run out the front door every time someone opens it, teach him to sit and stay whenever he approaches a doorway, and he will learn not to bolt when a door is open. Learning obedience cues is a positive outlet for his puppy energy.

When you teach a puppy basic cues, it helps stop problems from developing before they even start. If a behavior problem does develop, it will not be nearly as severe and will be much easier to fix with a dog who has received training from the outset.

The Basic Commands

It is important to realize that training is a process. Start off by using your training sessions to teach the exercises, and progress to practicing once the

Basic commands help you instill polite behavior, such as sitting and waiting for food, in your puppy.

behaviors have been taught. Initially, it is best to practice with your puppy every day for about ten to fifteen minutes. As your puppy matures, you can lengthen each practice session. If you prefer to do two shorter sessions that total ten to fifteen minutes each day, and you find that doing so fits your schedule better, the results will be the same. The best way to progress through the lessons is to practice one cue until your puppy recognizes and responds to it, and then build his repertoire by moving on to the next cue. The exercises in this chapter are presented in the suggested order in which they should be taught, though it's not necessary to proceed in this order if you choose otherwise.

Prepare for your training sessions with your puppy on leash and with his training collar on, and have treats handy. Pay attention to your timing and tone of voice, and be ready to reward your puppy enthusiastically as he learns each step of each cue.

Walking on Leash

Before you start your first heeling lesson, it is best to go through the motions without your puppy. The following are simple steps to get you started teaching your pup to walk on leash:

1. Stand up straight and relaxed, with your feet either together or shoulder-width apart.
2. Hold your arms down at your sides and relaxed.
3. Start walking while saying "Let's go." Do this for one minute, making sure that your left arm stays down and relaxed at your side.
4. Stop and give yourself a lot of praise!

To teach your puppy to walk on leash, begin with your puppy at your left side and with the leash in your right hand. Place your right thumb through the loop of the leash and gather up the rest of the leash in your right hand. You want to have some slack in the leash; it should not be so tight that you restrain the puppy. You may be inclined to hold the leash in your left hand, but you are less likely to restrain your puppy and tug him un-necessarily if you have the leash in your right hand.

Keep some training treats in your left hand (it also is easier to give the puppy treats from your left hand than your right) and tell the puppy "Let's go" as you start moving forward. Show your puppy a treat in your hand and allow your puppy to follow the treat. As soon as he takes a few steps, stop, praise and pet him, and then give him the treat. Then do it all again, starting with the verbal cue "Let's go." Practice for about ten minutes.

If your puppy starts to pull ahead of you, do an about turn (see "Walking on Leash" in chapter 6) so that you start walking in the opposite direction. If you keep changing direction on him, he will learn to watch you more closely and look to you for direction instead of trying to lead the way himself.

Some puppies will naturally tug while on leash. In fact, pulling has been bred into some dogs, such as the Siberian Husky and Bernese Mountain Dog, who were devised to pull sleds or carts. The breed of your puppy doesn't really matter in this regard, though, because as soon

Start your walk with your dog at your left side, waiting for you to set the pace of your movement.

as any dog feels a pull on his leash, his instinct is to pull against it. The key to training your puppy to walk on leash is to get his attention and make him understand that there's nothing more fun or fulfilling than walking by your side. Additionally, don't underestimate the value of talking to your puppy. Your encouraging, happy voice will add to the puppy's desire to please you and to walk attentively by your side.

As long as your puppy is walking next to you without running ahead, you can continue to give him treats, but start giving them less frequently. Make your puppy work a little harder each time for his reward, and stop using treats as the primary form of reward. As your puppy learns what is expected of him, you want him to start obeying you because he wants to, not just because there is food involved. If your puppy obeys only when a treat is at stake, it can create a multitude of problems down the road. You don't want to end up with a dog who listens only if he is hungry or who appears to be trained but will sometimes refuse the treat and do as he pleases as he matures and becomes more independent.

It is important to keep giving your puppy verbal and hands-on praise as you're weaning him off the treats. You want to appeal to all of the puppy's senses with your rewards: petting (touch), an upbeat tone of voice and "Good puppy" praise (hearing), your smile and happiness with him (sight), and treats (smell and taste).

Sometimes your puppy will lag behind you. The biggest mistake you can make is to stop and wait for him, as this will quickly teach him that he is in charge of what happens on a walk. If your puppy stops or lags behind, say "Let's go, good puppy" in a high-pitched, happy voice. Then start walking, taking small, quick steps and saying "Let's go. Good puppy" to encourage him along.

Still do your about turns if the puppy gets ahead of you. Anytime he moves away from the proper walking position, just give him a little tug to bring him back, tell him "Let's go," and keep walking. Every few minutes, stop to give him a lot of praise in the form of petting, clapping, and encouraging words.

Sit

The next exercise to teach is the *sit*, which is essential for good manners and usually easy to teach. Train your puppy to sit while waiting for his food to be served and at other times when you can practice at home and in the community.

Start by placing your right thumb through the loop of the leash and grasping the leash halfway down so it rests in the palm of your hand. There should be slack in the leash.

Stand in front of and facing your puppy with a treat in your right hand. Keep your right arm down, but let him see the treat. Lift your right hand, bend your arm, and say "Sit." If your puppy doesn't sit right away, place the treat in front of his nose and lift the treat in an arc over his head and toward his back. As he follows the treat, he will lift his muzzle; as his head goes up, his rear end should go down. Issue the verbal cue "Sit," and as soon as he sits, give him the treat and a lot of love and praise.

When luring your puppy into the *sit* position, you'll see his rear end go down as he looks up to follow the treat in your hand.

If your puppy tries to grab the treat out of your hand, close your hand tightly around the treat and wait for him to settle down before you try again. He is not allowed to take the treat while he is biting your hand, and you are not to give him the treat unless he responds correctly to your cue.

If your puppy doesn't respond to the treat, try holding your training session right before the puppy's dinnertime so that he is motivated to work for food. If your puppy is not food-motivated, try teaching him to sit by gently pulling up on the leash with your left hand while you gently lift up his muzzle with your right hand. When you lift the puppy's muzzle, it shifts the his weight, making him automatically lower his rear end into the *sit* position.

Timing is everything in training. Reward your puppy with a treat at the moment he reaches the proper position.

Sit/Stay

The *stay* command works in conjunction with other exercises, such as *sit*, *down*, and *stand*. When teaching the *stay*, you will work to increase both time and distance, but keep in mind that you want to build up the amount of time your puppy stays in position before you teach him to stay from a distance. Teaching the *stay* verbal cue is easiest when you begin with the puppy in the *sit* position (the *down/stay* and *stand/stay* are discussed later in this chapter).

Start by placing your puppy in the *sit* position next to you on your left-hand side. Hold the leash in your right hand and keep it nice and short. For this exercise, you want minimal slack in the leash so you can stop the puppy more quickly if he tries to get up from the *sit*.

When your puppy is in the *sit* position, place your left hand in front of his face, with your palm facing him, and tell him to "Stay." Step in front of the pup with your right foot and pivot so that you are now facing your puppy. Repeat "Stay," saying it quietly and drawing out the word.

Next, walk around the puppy and tell him to "Stay." Slowly and carefully walk around while quietly repeating and drawing out the word: "Staaay." As soon as you come full circle around your puppy, stop and give him a lot of praise.

Repeat the entire exercise. This time, when you pivot in front of him, take one step back. Make sure you don't let out too much leash at one time. You want to let the leash out very slowly so that if your puppy gets up from the *sit*, you can quickly bring the leash up, place him back into position, and say "Sit."

Start each exercise with the same hand signal as the puppy sits next to you. Each time you pivot in front of him, take another step back and then slowly move in toward him again, drawing out "Siiit, staaay." Once you are back in position, release your puppy from the *stay* by saying "OK" in a bright, upbeat tone, and give him a lot of praise.

Your hand signal as you issue the *stay* cue communicates that you want the puppy to remain in position.

With the *stay*, physical and verbal praise is more effective than food rewards because treats will often excite the dog and make him more likely to break the *stay*. To that end, calm body language is important while practicing this exercise.

As you back away from your puppy, stand tall with your shoulders squarely facing him. If you crouch down as you move away, you will seem much more approachable, and your puppy is more likely to break the *stay* and come to you.

As you continue to practice this for a few minutes each day, slowly increase the length of time that you keep your dog in the *stay* position. Once again, remember to build time in the *sit/stay* position before you build distance. In the AKC Canine Good Citizen test, handlers walk to the end of a 20-foot line while the dog stays. A three-minute *sit/stay* is the standard for the Companion Dog title in AKC obedience competition.

As you progress with the *stay*, keep taking one step backward each time you practice until you reach the end of the leash.

Come/Recall

The *come* cue, or recall, is an action command. When working on the *sit/stay*, you need to be calm and move slowly, but you should be much more animated when teaching your dog to come when called. As a matter of fact, the more animated you are, the better.

Get started by placing your puppy into the *sit/stay* position with him on leash and sitting at your side. Slowly walk to the end of the leash and turn and face your puppy. As in the *sit/stay*, stand tall and erect; a calm, assertive stance is important so that your puppy doesn't break the *sit/stay* until you give the signal.

Hold the leash and give the verbal cue "Come. Good puppy, come." At this point, you want to start running backward, letting your puppy catch up to you. Once he reaches you, crouch down and lavish him with praise.

Repeat this exercise over and over in each practice session, each time cheering the puppy on and making a big fuss when he gets to you. You want your puppy to know that he will receive a lot of praise every single time he comes to you. If for some reason he doesn't come right to you, keep backing up to encourage your puppy to run toward you, giving him praise once he reaches you.

Once your puppy is responding to the *come* cue consistently, you want to start working at a greater distance. Get a long leash, about 20 to 30 feet long. Put the leash on your puppy, take him to an open area, and let him sniff around and play for a bit. Once he becomes interested in something, give him a very happy-sounding cue: "Come, good puppy! Come, good puppy!" As he starts toward you, run backward and gather up the leash. He should keep coming toward you, but if he starts to deviate from his course, start moving in the opposite direction of your puppy and give the leash a little tug.

As soon as he gets to you, make a big fuss over him with physical and verbal praise. Be prepared to repeat this exercise many times. With consistent practice, your puppy should respond to the *come* cue every time. You must remember to call him each time he gets distracted so that you get his focus back on you. He must learn that coming to you

Encourage a reliable response by making your puppy's coming to you a positive experience each and every time.

when you call him takes precedence over anything else he may be doing at the time.

It is important to continue to practice this exercise on the long leash and around distractions until the puppy is responding reliably. Your puppy should come the first time you call him 100 percent of the time before you take this cue to the next level.

The next stage of this exercise is to bring your puppy to a small fenced area, remove his leash, and place him on a very light line (approximately 10 feet in length). The light line serves as your "emergency backup," to be used only if your puppy does not respond to your call. For the light line, you can use a light nylon rope, available from most hardware stores or home-supply outlets.

Practice from about 20 feet away from your puppy, letting him drag the line around. If your pup doesn't come on one of the occasions when you call him, slowly walk closer to him and call him again as you crouch down. If he still doesn't respond, reach out and take the line, run backwards, and bring him to you. You want to practice with the light line until you have 100 percent consistency for about a week.

Once you have that consistency, bring another dog into the fenced area and practice on the light line with this new distraction. When your dog is consistently responding despite the distraction, move to a larger fenced area and practice the entire routine from the beginning. Upon reaching the 100 percent consistency again, bring your dog back to the smaller fenced area and repeat the same routine but with no leash or line on your puppy.

Practice first without a distraction for about a week, and then with a distraction for a week. Later, you can introduce more and more distractions—food, cats, children, and so on—until you feel that your dog will reliably respond to your call at all times.

Always keep in mind that reliability should never replace caution. If you are in a new environment, keep the long line on the puppy as a backup should the new environment prove too much of a distraction. There is no harm in keeping your dog on a long leash when, for example, out hiking or at the beach. Do not ever rush to take the leash off your puppy. If you force this process, your runaway student may take a few hundred steps forward—and one big step backward in his training.

Down and Down/Stay

Place your puppy in a *sit* facing you, and hold the leash in your left hand and a treat in your right hand. Lift your right hand above his head and then move your hand down past his face, toward the floor, calmly and quietly saying "Dowwwwnnn." As you bring your right hand down, your puppy will follow your hand, knowing that the treat is in it. Once your hand reaches the ground, he will start sniffing your hand, trying to get the treat. As long as both of his elbows and his rear end are down, you can give him the treat, followed by that ever-effective verbal and physical praise.

Make sure that your puppy doesn't bring his hindquarters up when his head goes down; you want to praise him only when his whole body is in the *down* position. After doing this three to five times, take a break and do something else, such as practicing the recall.

The *down* position is a very submissive position, and it tends to be the most difficult of all exercises to teach, which is why you need to start teaching it while your puppy is still very young and trusting. Most dogs, no matter how sweet and docile they are, won't

While your puppy may lie down on his own to relax, he's likely to resist assuming the *down* position when he's told to do it.

"submit" if they don't have to. Most dogs will resist at first—even more so if they sense that their owners are hesitant about enforcing the command. If you are not sure of yourself, your puppy will sense your lack of confidence and will challenge you when he does not want to do something that you've asked him to do.

It is important with the *down*, much more so than with the other exercises, that you start using treats intermittently as quickly as you start using them. In other words, start weaning your puppy off of food rewards as soon as you get a proper response from him. Use treats sporadically, but let your puppy work mainly for your praise and the enjoyment of a job well done. If you rely on treats in the beginning, you will have more difficulty later getting your puppy to obey this command.

If your puppy is not responding to the *down* cue, you can help him along a little with some extra guidance. Place your puppy in a *sit/stay* on your left side. Gather the leash in your right hand and lift your left hand above your puppy's head. Move your left hand slowly down in front of your puppy's face. As you do this, say "Dowwwnnn" very slowly and quietly.

Once you get your puppy moving into the *down* position without popping back up immediately, you can begin working on the *down/stay*. Like the *sit/stay*, the *down/stay* is a helpful exercise for times when you want your dog to relax and stay put; for example, when you're eating dinner and you want him to lie at your feet or in a designated area until you're finished. Make certain that his *sit/stay* is reliable before expecting him to do a *down/stay*.

When starting the *down/stay*, you'll be very close to your puppy when you issue the cue.

To teach the *down/stay*, tell your puppy to "Stay" and show him your hand signal. Keep repeating the cue and showing him the *stay* hand signal. After a minute, release him and give him a lot of praise. Repeat this two more times, making each subsequent exercise last a bit longer than the previous one. In AKC Canine Good Citizen classes, you'll cue your puppy to stay as you walk to the end of a 20-foot line and return. If you go on to compete in obedience, you'll eventually build your dog up to a five-minute *down/stay*.

To condition your puppy to do a nice, steady *down/stay*, teach him to tolerate people walking over him while he stays in position. Once he will stay in the *down* position on his own, stand behind him and

With any type of *stay*, keep your hand signal in place as you increase the time and your distance from the dog.

step over his back from side to side. Once be becomes accustomed to your stepping over him, you can then straddle him and walk from his back to his front. Step on the leash as you do this to prevent him from getting up. This is a great exercise for your puppy because it conditions him to stay in position despite people walking near him and helps him become less startled by anyone, such as a child, running up to him. You'll also know that if your dog is sound asleep on the floor and blocking your path, you can easily step over him without worrying that he will jump up, trip you, and send you flying.

Go to Your Place

The *go to your place* cue is an easy skill to teach. Start by deciding on a spot in your house that will be the puppy's special place. This is the spot where he will go to relax during your dinnertime, when you have guests, and at any other time you don't want him underfoot but don't need him to be in his crate.

Put the leash on your puppy, get behind him, and start herding him toward his place. (*Herding* simply means keeping the puppy between you and his place.) Walk behind him, nudging him in the right direction if necessary, while saying "Go to your place. Go to your place. Good puppy." Once he gets there, stop and give him a lot of praise.

Each time you practice, start a little farther away from the puppy's place. Repeat the exercise several times a day and stop when your puppy is responding well. Start practicing without a leash when the puppy performs well with the leash on. You can teach other cues, such as *go to your crate*, the same way.

Leave It

The *leave it* cue can be taught easily while you are walking your puppy down the street or at home with a forbidden item, such as your shoes, that he loves to chew on. Keep the leash on your puppy when introducing this exercise. When he starts to go toward something he finds on the ground or toward the forbidden object, avert his attention with a squeaky toy and tell him to "Leave it." Once he ignores the item and looks at you, give him a lot of verbal and physical praise and then bring him back to the item and repeat.

Once he starts ignoring the object, move on to a more exciting object, such as a piece of chicken that you've dropped on the floor. If he even looks at the chicken, squeak your distracting toy and tell him to "Leave it." When he ignores the chicken, reward him with a lot of praise and a short play session with the squeaky toy.

Practice *leave it* each day. How long it takes to learn this cue varies among puppies, but soon your puppy will no longer acknowledge an object when you say "Leave it."

Stand and Stand/Stay

You can start this exercise with the puppy in either a *sit* or a *stand* position. To get your puppy to stand from a sitting position, hold a treat in front of his nose with your right hand. Gently touch his belly with the fingertips of your left hand and tickle him. As you tickle him, move the treat slightly so that he has to lean forward to follow it and, in doing so, bring up his hindquarters. However, don't bring it so far forward that he has to take a few steps to reach it.

The *stand/stay* is taught in the same basic way as the *sit/stay* and the *down/stay*.

As your puppy starts to stand, give him the verbal cue "Stand." Draw out the word, saying it slowly and quietly. When he is in a standing position, place the palm of your hand in front of his face and say "Stand, stay. Stay." Release him with "OK" and give him praise. Start off doing this exercise just twice.

As you progress to more repetitions of this cue, lengthen the time tof the *stay* before you release your puppy. The best way to do this is to gradually increase the number of times that you say "Stay." When he is staying for about a minute, you can give the verbal cue less often.

At that point, you can also start to move away from your puppy so that you are building distance as well as time. Build the distance literally a step at a time: take one step back, build up to a minute, take another step back, build up to a minute, and so on.

Don't try to accomplish everything all at once; practice for a few minutes each day. If you practice this exercise on a tabletop or another raised surface, it will help prepare the puppy for being placed on the examination table at the vet's office or for being groomed on a grooming table.

The *stand/stay* is necessary for any dog who's groomed on a table.

Teaching Your Puppy to Retrieve

Retrieving can be very easy with some breeds, such as Goldens, Labradors, and other retrievers, yet more challenging with others. Assess your puppy's natural inclination for retrieving by taking him for a walk in the park and throwing some sticks and balls around to gauge his reaction. The retrieve is a self-rewarding behavior and something that some dogs learn quite easily. If he doesn't pick up anything that you throw for him, tease him a little with one of the objects and praise him if he puts it in his mouth. Once you've determined that your puppy has an interest in retrieving, you can start teaching him as follows:

1. Choose a toy that your puppy really likes.
2. Toss the toy and encourage him to bring it back to you.
3. When the puppy brings the toy back to you, exchange it for a treat.
4. Practice this frequently until the puppy is responding consistently with his new retrieving skill.

Your local AKC-affiliated training club can help you get involved with more advanced activities involving retrieval, such as hunting tests and field trials. It is great exercise, and many dogs find these sports to be a lot of fun. Contact your local breed club or visit www.akc.org for more information.

A bumper is often used to stimulate a dog's retrieving instincts.

FUN AND GAMES

There are so many games you can play with your puppy—keep-away, follow the leader (with and without the leash), hide and seek, find the treat, and fetch are just a few examples. Games are fun and can be great training tools as well. They teach the puppy to focus on you, and they help stimulate his mind in an informal way.

For example, when you play keep-away, take the puppy's favorite toy and let him chase you to get it. Let the pup see you switch the toy from hand to hand and then hide it behind your back so that he learns to pay attention and watch you to figure out where the toy is. Give the puppy the toy and let him play with it before you take it back and start the game again. Just make certain that you do not tease him so much that he becomes frustrated with the game. If he does, he may jump up on you, nip you, or try to grab at your clothing.

Working on a few tricks with your puppy is another great way to have fun with him. In doing this, you're instilling basic obedience and teaching him behaviors that can be both useful and entertaining.

CHAPTER 10

Activities to Enjoy with Your Dog

A happy dog is an active dog. Boredom is every dog's worst enemy, and most purebred dogs were devised to perform specific tasks. Dogs really want to work for a living, whether it's gathering sheep, retrieving fallen ducks, or guarding an estate. Unemployment has been a big problem in the dog world for the past century, and few dogs get to spend their days doing what they were bred to do. The lucky dogs who are working full time today come mainly from the Toy Group, as these breeds were designed to be companions first and foremost and still make wonderful best friends.

In fact, all dogs today are serving humans as companions first, and, as such, participate with us in much of what we do, including yard work, walks on the beach, or rides to the market. Thanks to the AKC, there are plenty of activities that have been created just for dogs, too, and getting involved in some of these activities is guaranteed to make your dog smile.

Keeping your dog active gives him the physical and mental stimulation that he needs for good health and fulfillment.

Participating in activities gives our dogs the physical and mental exercise that they need to lead healthy and motivated lives. There are many different kinds of organized sports in which you and your dog can train and compete for ribbons and titles. Your dog can accompany you in activities that you already enjoy, and you'll also find plenty of things to do with your dog around the house and in your community. Participating in activities together is a wonderful way to bond with your dog, give him a job to do, and give him a full life.

AKC Events

The American Kennel Club hosts many types of competitive events for dogs. Conformation shows—commonly referred to as "dog shows"—measure how well purebred dogs conform to the official standards for their respective breeds. There are other AKC events that are open to all purebred and mixed-breed dogs that are registered or listed with the AKC regardless of their breeds, and there are also events specifically designed for certain types of dogs, such as sighthounds or retrievers, to develop and assess the skills for which they historically have been bred. When you find a sport that interests you, order the rules handbook from the AKC for that particular event; it will tell you all you need to know to get started. You can also research your chosen sport online at the AKC's website, www. akc.org, or contact your local breed club for more information.

Conformation Shows

More than just beauty contests for dogs, conformation shows determine how closely your dog resembles the ideal specimen of his breed in looks, temperament, and movement.

From local shows to major exhibitions, such as the AKC/Eukanuba National Championship, conformation is an exciting sport on all levels of competition.

Each dog in competition is evaluated by a judge against the standard for his breed, which dictates the essence of the breed, the breed's physical characteristics, and the work or purpose for which the breed was bred.

Conformation showing is very competitive. You will have to devote a lot of time and travel to the sport, and you may need to hire a professional handler to help you. You will also want to keep a close relationship with your breeder, who will be a wonderful resource to help you succeed in this time-honored and exciting sport.

There are several types of shows in which your puppy can compete: an all-breed show is open to all AKC-recognized breeds; a specialty show is specific to one breed; and a Group show is one where all of the breeds in a particular group (e.g., Sporting Group, Hound Group) are eligible to compete. There is a nonregular class for puppies between four and six months of age, and the following regular classes of competition at shows:

- The Puppy Class is for dogs between six and twelve months of age who are not yet champions.
- The Twelve- to Eighteen-Month Class is for dogs of this age range who are not yet champions.

A good breeder keeps his or her eye on the puppies from birth to evaluate them for show potential as they grow.

BE A PAL!

If you have an AKC-recognized breed but your puppy is not registrable with the AKC because his parents weren't AKC-registered or his litter wasn't registered by the breeder, or maybe because he's a rescue pup without papers, fear not, you and your buddy can still participate in AKC events. The AKC's Purebred Alternative Listing/Indefinite Listing Privilege (PAL/ILP) program allows unregistered dogs of AKC breeds to compete in both performance and companion events. All breeds can participate in events such as agility, tracking, obedience, rally, and even Junior Showmanship. The form to apply for the Purebred Alternative Listing/Indefinite Listing Privilege can be downloaded or obtained by emailing PAL@akc.org. When requesting a form via e-mail, please include your name and mailing address. Once enrolled in the PAL/ILP program, you can enter your "PAL" in AKC events just as easily as you can with a registrable dog. When filling out your entry form for events, use your dog's PAL/ILP number instead of his AKC registration number.

- The Novice Class is for dogs six months old or older who have no championship points and who have not won three first prizes in Novice or a first prize in the Bred-by-Exhibitor, American-Bred, or Open Classes.
- The Amateur-Owner-Handler Class is for dogs who are six months of age or older, are not champions, and who are handled by their owners (who have never been professional handlers or judges).
- The Bred-by-Exhibitor Class is for dogs who are not yet champions and are shown by their breeders/owners.
- The American-Bred Class is for dogs who were bred and born in the United States and are not yet champions.
- The Open Class is for any dog of at least six months of age.

The dogs who place first in their classes return to the ring to compete against each other. They are judged first against the others of their own sex; the winning male is awarded Winners Dog, and the winning female is awarded Winners Bitch. The Winners Dog and Winners Bitch then compete against all champions entered for the Best of Breed award. At the conclusion of Best of Breed judging, there are three placements awarded: Best of Breed (first place, regardless of sex), Best of Winners (the best dog of the Winners Dog and Winners Bitch), and Best of Opposite Sex (the best dog of the sex opposite to the Best of Breed winner).

In an all-breed show, the Best of Breed winners from each breed then compete against all of the other Best of Breed winners in their groups (i.e., all Toy Group winners compete together). There are four placements—Group One through Group Four—in Group judging. The Group One (first place) winners from each group then compete against each other for Best in Show. Out of the seven dogs in contention for Best in Show, only one placement is given. Best in Show accolades are what all breeders and handlers dream about.

When you choose a breeder, let him or her know that you want to pursue conformation showing with your puppy so that the breeder can help you pick out a good show prospect. Read and know the breed standard inside and out; become familiar with both the desirable and the undesirable traits for the show ring. Go to shows and watch other dogs of your breed. Teach your puppy how to stand and stay for the judge, and take him to conformation classes as soon as possible so that you both learn about ring procedure and etiquette. All of these components, along with becoming active in your local all-breed club, will help get you started successfully in the wonderful world of dog shows. And who knows? You may someday end up winning the AKC/Eukanuba National Championship!

Obedience Trials

Unlike training your pet to obey basic obedience cues, the training for competitive obedience is more regimented. There are three levels of obedience competition—Novice, Open, and Utility—that progress in difficulty. Dogs who are successful at the highest levels of obedience can work toward the Obedience Trial Champion title. Competing in obedience has given many young handlers a start in careers as dog trainers.

If you have a purebred dog who doesn't have the proper documentation to be registered with the AKC, or if you have a mixed-breed dog, you can still list your dog with the AKC's PAL (for purebreds) or Canine Partners (for mixed breeds) programs so that he will be eligible for obedience competition. The training you do with your puppy at home, such as the *come*, the *sit/stay*, and retrieving games, start laying the foundation for obedience. In addition, any puppy who participates in the AKC S.T.A.R. Puppy® Program and goes on to earn his Canine Good Citizen title has an excellent head start in obedience competition.

Beginner Novice is the first level of obedience, with all exercises done on leash. Next is Novice, and at this level, your dog must heel and walk in a figure eight on leash, keeping to your pace; off-leash heeling is also tested. He must stand and stay for an examination while you walk away and the judge touches the dog's head, body, and hindquarters. You must demonstrate the recall (or *come*) and your dog must do a one-minute *sit/stay* and a three-minute *down/stay* with you on the opposite side of the ring.

Once your dog earns a qualifying score at the Novice level three times, he earns the Companion Dog (CD) title. On any paperwork regarding your dog, you will be able to place the CD suffix after his name.

Retrieving a dumbbell is among the advanced skills that are tested in obedience competition.

Various jumps are part of agility (shown here) and obedience trials.

The Open level is the intermediate level of obedience competition. Exercises include the heeling and figure eight from the Novice class, but they are done off leash in Open. The drop-on-recall exercise requires you to call your dog from across the ring and issue the *down* cue as he's coming toward you, at which point the dog must drop into the *down* position and then, when commanded, get up and resume coming to you.

Retrieving and jumping exercises are also introduced at this level. The dog must retrieve a dumbbell on flat ground, over a high jump, and over a broad jump that measures twice as long as the dog is tall. The *sit/stay* is increased to three minutes and the *down/stay* is increased to five minutes. At the Open level, you need to have more off-leash control and rely more on hand and voice signals because the dog is tested on working at a distance from you. The title available at the Open level is Companion Dog Excellent (CDX).

The highest level of obedience competition is the Utility level. In Utility competition, you revisit some of the basic cues, and some of the exercises are done with hand signals only. You also direct your dog with hand signals at a distance to retrieve a glove; the change in the item retrieved is significant because teaching a dog to retrieve items of different textures and weights requires additional training.

In the directed-jumping exercise, you send the dog away from you and indicate which of two jumps he is to jump over. One of the tougher exercises is the moving stand and examination, in which the dog must heel, stop in his tracks at your cue, and stay standing for an examination from the judge, all while you keep moving forward. The dog must return to you on your cue after the judge has finished his examination. The titles available at the Utility level are Utility Dog (UD) and Utility Dog Excellent (UDX).

In order to receive a qualifying score at any level, your dog must pass with at least 170 out of a possible 200 points, while scoring at least half of the available points for each exercise. When your dog earns a passing score, he receives what's known as a "leg," and three legs are required for the title at each level.

AKC Rally®

An enjoyable precursor to obedience competition is AKC Rally® competition. Rally involves obedience; however, the regulations and judging are not nearly as strict or as precise as in traditional obedience. Instead of a judge directing you through the exercises, you and your dog walk a course that includes ten to twenty stations, depending on the level of competition. A sign at each station tells you what exercise (*sit/stay, come, down*, and other cues and variations thereof) to perform at that station. You move through the course at your own pace, and unlimited communication with your dog is allowed; this means that you can use hand signals, verbal cues, clapping—whatever is needed to get the message across.

A local AKC obedience club is the best resource for Rally classes and competition training. Rally is also a great introductory sport for young people who want to get started in organized competition and eventually progress to competing at higher levels with their dogs.

Agility Trials

Agility competition has quickly risen in popularity in the United States. The agility course is like an amusement park for dogs. It is challenging without being too intense, it stimulates their minds by offering plenty of new things to learn, and it boosts their confidence by working their bodies in unique ways. There is no sport that brings a nervous, fearful, and insecure dog out of his shell faster than agility.

The obstacles on an agility course include various types of tunnels and jumps, weave poles, teeter-totters, A-frames, and other physical challenges that test a dog's balance and athleticism. The jump heights are adjusted based on the height of the dog competing.

Handlers accompany their dogs on the course, running beside the dogs to direct them through the obstacles in the correct order; all handling is done off leash. Runs are scored based on both speed and accuracy. Precision factors, such as whether the dog displaces a bar or panel on a jump, touches the contact zones upon entering and exiting certain obstacles, or leaves the "pause table" before being released, affect his score.

Border Collies are among the speedy, athletic breeds who fare well on the agility course.

A Shetland Sheepdog enjoys the fast pace of agility competition as he bursts out of the open tunnel.

There are three levels of competition in agility—Novice, Open, and Excellent—each progressively more difficult than the previous. The Novice-level course contains fourteen to sixteen obstacles. The Open level is for dogs who have completed the Novice level; there are sixteen to eighteen obstacles on the course, which includes more turns and twists and is more complicated overall. After success in the Open level, dogs graduate to the highest level, Excellent. There are eighteen to twenty obstacles on the Excellent course. Teamwork is of utmost importance at all levels of competition, but especially so at this level, as the dog must follow mostly verbal cues rather than physical guidance from his handler. The handler also typically issues cues at a greater distance from the dog at the Excellent level.

The newest class, known as FAST (Fifteen And Send Time), challenges owners and dogs to be both fast and strategic. The class includes fifteen obstacles, each assigned a point value, but there is no order to the course, meaning dog and owner can tackle the obstacles in any order. The class also includes a distance challenge that must be completed properly for a qualifying run.

It is very easy to start training dogs in agility because it is so much fun for them. Dogs of any breed, size, and personality type can be successful in this sport. You can buy or make equipment rather inexpensively for practice at home, or if your backyard is too small, there are agility clubs throughout the country, many of which have obstacle courses to practice on.

Before you start formal training, you can first use items found around the home to get your puppy used to some of the maneuvers required in agility on a smaller scale. For example, hold a hula hoop a few inches above the ground and encourage your puppy to jump through it. Help your puppy get up on a low table and teach him to stay there until you release him. You will need to get him used to a variety of new skills while incorporating his knowledge of basic obedience to ease his entry into this fun and exciting sport.

As you progress with training, you are in essence building your dog into a true athlete, so you must discuss with your veterinarian when your puppy can start more vigorous jumping and what you should be feeding him. When competing in agility, you will be running with your dog, so you should also become more fit as a result.

Tracking

All dogs and owners can participate in tracking, an enjoyable activity that fully utilizes and enhances the scenting ability that all canines possess. The dog's sense of smell is unfathomable compared to a human's; it is reported to be 100,000 times stronger. Training a dog to track is one of the most fascinating and invigorating activities that you can do with your dog. Some owners get involved in tracking just for the fun and satisfaction of training, competing, and earning titles with their dogs, while others seek to lay the foundation for more advanced training, such as search and rescue, bomb detection, and drug detection work.

Scenthounds are known as the "nosiest" breeds, but all dogs have amazing scenting capabilities and the potential to do well in tracking.

In tracking competition, a human lays the scent track, and items such as gloves or wallets are placed along the track for the dog to find. The titles available are Tracking Dog (TD), Tracking Dog Excellent (TDX), and Variable Surface Tracking (VST), each having a progressively more difficult track. Tracks vary in length and range from basic straight paths and easy turns to complicated twists, changes of direction, and decoy paths. Variable Surface Tracking requires a dog to follow a trail over different surfaces, including one that is devoid of vegetation, such as a concrete sidewalk. Tracking competitions are usually held at daybreak, as the cooler morning temperatures keep the tracks fresh and still.

Any dog can be trained for tracking; however, some of the breeds more commonly seen in competition include the German Shepherd Dog, Golden Retriever, Labrador Retriever, and a variety of the scenthound breeds. You can get started in tracking by contacting a local tracking club; find one near you on the American Kennel Club's website (www.akc.org).

Earthdog Tests

Earthdog tests give terrier breeds and Dachshunds the opportunity to test their hunting skills, or "go to ground," on quarry such as rats and woodchucks, small vermin that they were traditionally bred to hunt. The animals used in these tests are well cared for and are kept caged so that the dogs never make contact with them. They are simply used so that the dogs can track their scent underground.

If you have an eligible breed and want to gauge your dog's interest in the sport, take him to a wooded area where there are rabbits and squirrels. Put your puppy on a 30-foot-long leash, which will allow him the freedom to move around, yet still afford you complete control over him. Let him sniff the ground while you encourage him to use his nose by saying in a low, happy tone, "Find the rabbit! Where is the rabbit?"

Contact your local breed club to find out about earthdog training in your area so that you can become involved and start preparing your puppy for future competition.

Hunt Tests and Field Trials

It is often confusing for the novice owner to understand the difference between hunt tests and field trials. The hunt test is the first step; it is an independent, pass-or-fail test that simulates a hunting situation and evaluates your dog's natural desire to hunt. In field trials, which require more advanced training, dogs compete against each other and receive points toward their titles.

Field trials and hunt tests are offered for pointing breeds, retrievers, and spaniels with the intent of testing a dog's ability to find game and point, retrieve, or flush the game, depending on his breed's bred-for function. The dogs must work efficiently and freely, in cooperation with their handlers. To compete, a dog of an eligible breed must be at least six months old.

Decoys are used in training to simulate real hunting situations.

To prepare for hunt tests and field trials, your young pup needs strong obedience skills. He needs to come when called from a distance, retrieve, and respond to whistle cues telling him to turn around and return to you. Your pup will also need a very steady *sit/stay* so that he stays close to you during competition until you release him.

Start by getting involved with your local breed club or with an AKC-affiliated performance club (search at www.akc.org); some of these clubs offer training classes. You'll also be able to meet people who are training and/or competing with their dogs in hunting and field events. You may even find a mentor who will help you become more involved as a member of the club and a competitive dog owner.

Dachshund Field Trials

The very first Dachshund field trial was held in 1935, and ever since, the Dachshund has competed with utmost tenacity and courage. Dogs are judged on their ability to track a scent and their willingness and determination to chase the rabbit down. For example, if the rabbit runs into a drain pipe or burrow in which the Dachshund can fit, he must continue the chase.

Like Beagles and Basset Hounds in their breeds' field trials, Dachshunds also compete in pairs, or *braces*—however, they tend to be a bit less vocal when on a "hot" trail.

It doesn't matter if you have a longhaired, wirehaired, or smooth Dachshund to compete. Even Miniature Dachshunds can compete and do so with much enthusiasm. The only prerequisite is that your Dachshund is registered with the AKC and is at least six months old.

Lure Coursing

Lure coursing is a captivating sport that was traditionally open to sighthound breeds only, but a program called the Coursing Ability Test (CAT) now brings the sport to all breeds and even mixed breeds. For all of these events, dogs must be at least one year of age.

Lure coursing events are held in open fields, and the dogs chase artificial lures to mimic the prey that sighthounds typically hunt, such as rabbits. The dogs are judged on their speed, agility, and ability to follow the lure, among other factors, as they race and zigzag across the field. A chase usually lasts anywhere from forty-five seconds to three minutes.

Earning titles in the CAT requires a dog to pass the test multiple times. For example, three passes earn the Coursing Ability (CA) title; ten passes earn the Coursing Ability Advanced (CAA) title; twenty-five passes earn the Coursing Ability Excellent (CAX) title; and fifty passes earn the Coursing Ability Excellent 2 (CAX2) title.

In regular lure coursing events, sighthounds are eligible to compete and win titles. A dog earns a Junior Courser (JC) title by passing two tests on a 600-yard course with four turns under two different judges. A Senior Courser (SC) title is earned after passing four tests, run with at least one other dog, under two different judges. The most competitive

Training for water retrieves is part of the preparation for retriever field trials, and the competitors are more than happy to oblige!

It's exciting to see a dog's natural instincts come to the fore in competitive trials designed for certain breeds.

title in lure coursing is Master Courser (MC), earned after achieving Senior Courser and passing at least twenty-five tests.

These tests are held all over the United States, but, of course, most are held in remote areas. Your national breed club can direct you to the best place for lure coursing testing and training nearest you. Connecting and networking with your breed club, both local and national, is the key to success in any competitive dog event.

Herding

Herding tests and trials are based on a dog's natural instinct with livestock. This sport is open to the many breeds that have traditionally been used for herding or otherwise show some natural ability in the field. All of the breeds in the Herding Group, plus the Bernese Mountain Dog, Giant Schnauzer, Rottweiler, Samoyed, Soft Coated Wheaten Terrier, and several others, are eligible to compete in the Herding Instinct Test starting at six months of age and all other herding events and tests starting at nine months of age.

The Herding Instinct Test is a noncompetitive test that evaluates a dog's basic ability to move and control livestock. For this first test, your dog does not have to be trained; the test simply gauges the propensity of your dog for herding. If successful in the Herding Instinct Test, your puppy can then move on to advanced training, and eventually into herding tests and competitive herding trials.

To be qualified as Herding Tested (HT), the first title achieved in herding, a dog must pass the basic herding test twice under two different judges. To pass the test, the dog has ten minutes to quietly and calmly move the livestock from one pylon to another pylon and back again while following basic herding cues from his owner. The course runs anywhere from 100 to 200 feet in length. As the dog moves into higher levels of competition and toward his Herding Trial Champion certificate, the course becomes more difficult, involving more turns and moving livestock into smaller, more varied areas. Commonly used livestock include ducks, sheep, and cattle.

Drafting and Carting

Do you have a draft dog, such as a Bernese Mountain Dog, Mastiff, Saint Bernard, Bouvier des Flandres, Greater Swiss Mountain Dog, or Rottweiler? Drafting, or carting, as it is commonly known, is something that you can teach your dog for competition or simply to give the dog a job to do, no matter where you live. Your dog will feel useful and burn some energy, and you will have the satisfaction of teaching him something helpful to you. Imagine how proud your dog would be if he could help bring firewood to the house in his cart—and how grateful you would be that you didn't have to carry all of that wood! The national parent clubs of these six breeds sponsor drafting tests, and the AKC recognizes and records the titles awarded at these tests.

Draft-dog skills aren't just for competition, they can be used for fun, too!

Resources

Books

The American Kennel Club's Meet the Breeds: Dog Breeds from A to Z

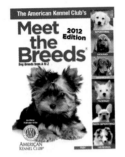

(Irvine, California: BowTie Press, 2011) The ideal puppy buyer's guide, the 2012 edition of this book has all you need to know about each AKC-recognized and Miscellaneous Class breed.

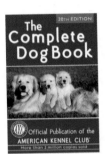

The Complete Dog Book,

20th edition (New York: Ballantine Books, 2006) This official publication of the AKC, first published in 1929, includes the complete histories and breed standards of 153 recognized breeds as well as information on general care and the dog sport.

The Complete Dog Book for Kids (New York:

Howell Book House, 1996) Specifically geared toward young people, this official publication of the AKC presents 149 breeds and varieties as well as introductory owners' information.

Citizen Canine: Ten Essential Skills Every Well-Mannered Dog Should Know by

Mary R. Burch, PhD (Freehold, New Jersey: Kennel Club Books, 2010) This official AKC publication is the definitive guide to the AKC's Canine Good Citizen® program, recognized as the gold standard of behavior for dogs, with more than half a million dogs trained.

DOGS: The First 125 Years of the American Kennel Club

(Freehold, New Jersey: Kennel Club Books, 2009) This official AKC publication presents an authoritative, complete history of the AKC, including detailed information not found in any other volume.

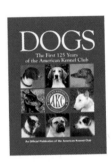

Dog Heroes of September 11th: A Tribute to America's Search and Rescue Dogs,

tenth-anniversary edition, by Nona Kilgore Bauer (Freehold, New Jersey: Kennel Club Books, 2011) A publication to salute the canines that served in the recovery missions following the 9/11 terrorist attacks, this book serves as a lasting tribute to these noble American heroes.

The Original Dog Bible: The Definitive Source for All Things Dog, 2nd edition,

by Kristin Mehus-Roe (Irvine, California: BowTie Press, 2009) This 831-page magnum opus

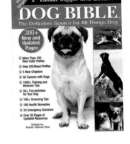

includes more than 250 breed profiles, hundreds of color photographs, and a wealth of information on every dog topic imaginable—thousands of practical tips on grooming, training, care, and much more.

Periodicals

American Kennel Club Gazette

Every month since 1889, serious dog fanciers have looked to the *AKC Gazette* for authoritative advice on training, showing, breeding, and canine health. Each issue includes the breed columns section, written by experts from the respective breed clubs. Only available electronically.

AKC Family Dog

This is a bimonthly magazine for the dog lover whose special dog is "just a pet." Helpful tips, how-tos, and features are written in an entertaining and reader-friendly format. It's a lifestyle magazine for today's busy families who want to enjoy rewarding, mutually happy relationships with their canine companions.

Dog Fancy

The world's most widely read dog magazine, *Dog Fancy* celebrates dogs and the people who love them. Each monthly issue includes info on cutting-edge medical developments, health and fitness (with a focus on prevention, treatment, and natural therapy), behavior and training, travel and activities, breed profiles, dog news, and issues and trends for owners of purebred and mixed-breed dogs. The magazine informs, inspires, and entertains while promoting responsible dog ownership. Throughout its more than forty-year history, *Dog Fancy* has garnered numerous honors, including being named the Best All-Breed Magazine by the Dog Writers Association of America.

Dog World

With more than ninety-five years of tradition as the top magazine for active people with active dogs, *Dog World* provides authoritative, valuable, and entertaining content to the community of serious dog enthusiasts and participants, including breeders; conformation exhibitors; obedience, agility, herding, and field trial competitors; veterinarians; groomers; and trainers. This monthly magazine is the resource to turn to for up-to-date information about canine health, advanced training, holistic and homeopathic methods, breeding, and conformation and performance sports.

Dogs in Review

For more than fifteen years, *Dogs in Review* has showcased the finest dogs in the United States and from around the world. The emphasis has always been on strong editorial content, with input from distinguished breeders, judges, and handlers worldwide. This global perspective distinguishes this monthly publication from its competitors—no other North American dog-show magazine gathers together so many international experts to enlighten and entertain its readership.

Dogs USA

Dogs USA is an annual lifestyle magazine published by the editors of *Dog Fancy* that covers all aspects of the dog world: culture, art, history, travel, sports, and science. It also profiles breeds to help prospective owners choose the best dogs for their future needs, such as a potential show champion, super service dog, great pet, or competitive star.

Natural Dog

Natural Dog is the magazine dedicated to giving a dog a natural lifestyle. From nutritional choices to grooming to dog-supply options, this publication helps readers make the transition from traditional to natural methods. The magazine also explores the array of complementary treatments available for today's dogs: acupuncture, massage, homeopathy, aromatherapy, and much more. *Natural Dog* appears as an annual publication and also as the flip side of *Dog Fancy* magazine four times a year (in February, May, August, and November).

Puppies USA

Also from the editors of *Dog Fancy,* this annual magazine offers essential information for all new puppy owners. *Puppies USA* is lively and informative, including advice on general care, nutrition, grooming, and training techniques for all puppies, whether purebred or mixed breed, adopted, rescued, or purchased. In addition, it offers family fun through quizzes, contests, and much more. An extensive breeder directory is included.

Websites

www.akc.org

The American Kennel Club's website is an excellent starting point for researching dog breeds and learning about puppy care. The site lists hundreds of breeders, along with basic information about breed selection and basic care. The site also has links to the national breed club of every AKC-recognized breed; breed-club sites offer plenty of detailed breed information, as well as lists of member breeders. In addition, you can find the AKC National Breed Club Rescue List at www.akc.org/breeds/rescue.cfm. If looking for purebred puppies, go to www.puppybuyerinfo.com for AKC classifieds and parent club referrals.

www.dogchannel.com

Dog Channel is "the website for dog lovers," where hundreds of thousands of visitors each month find extensive information on breeds, training, health and nutrition, puppies, care, activities, and more. Interactive features include forums, Dog College, games, puzzles, and Club Dog, an exclusive free club where dog lovers can create blogs for their pets and earn points to buy products. DogChannel is the definitive one-stop site for all things dog.

www.meetthebreeds.com

This is the official website of the AKC Meet the Breeds® event, hosted by the American Kennel Club at the Jacob Javits Center in New York City in the fall. The first Meet the Breeds event took place in 2009. The website includes information on every recognized breed of dog and cat, alphabetically listed, as well as the breeders, demonstration facilitators, sponsors, and vendors participating in the annual event.

AKC Affiliates

The **AKC Museum of the Dog**,
established in 1981, is located in St. Louis, Missouri, and houses the world's finest collection of art devoted to the dog. Visit www.museumofthedog.org.

The **AKC Humane Fund**
promotes the joy and value of responsible and productive pet ownership through education, outreach, and grant-making. Monies raised may fund grants to organizations that teach responsible pet ownership, provide for the health and well-being of all dogs, and preserve and celebrate the human-animal bond and the evolutionary relationship between dogs and humankind. Go to www.akchumanefund.org.

The **American Kennel Club Companion Animal Recovery (CAR) Corporation** is dedicated to
reuniting lost microchipped and tattooed pets with their owners. AKC CAR maintains a permanent-identification database and provides lifetime recovery services 24 hours a day, 365 days a year, for all animal species. Millions of pets are enrolled in the program, which was established in 1995. Visit www.akccar.org.

The **American Kennel Club Canine Health Foundation (AKC CHF), Inc.** is the largest
foundation in the world to fund canine-only health studies for purebred and mixed-breed dogs. More than $22 million has been allocated in research funds to more than 500 health studies conducted to help dogs live longer, healthier lives. Go to www.akcchf.org.

AKC Programs

The **Canine Good Citizen Program (CGC)** was established in 1989 and is designed to recognize dogs that have good manners at home and in the
community. This rapidly growing, nationally recognized program stresses responsible dog ownership for owners and basic training and good manners for dogs. All dogs who pass the ten-step Canine Good Citizen test receive a certificate from the American Kennel Club. Go to www.akc.org/events/cgc.

The **AKC S.T.A.R. Puppy Program** is designed to get dog owners and their puppies off to a good start and is aimed at loving dog owners who have taken the time to attend basic
obedience classes with their puppies. After completing a six-week training course, the puppy must pass the AKC S.T.A.R. Puppy test, which evaluates **s**ocialization, **t**raining, **a**ctivity, and **r**esponsibility. Go to www.akc.org/starpuppy.

The **AKC Therapy Dog Program** recognizes all American Kennel Club dogs and their owners who have given their time and helped people by volunteering as therapy dog-and-owner teams. The AKC Therapy Dog Program awards an official American Kennel Club title to dogs who have worked to improve the lives of the people they have visited. The AKC Therapy Dog title (AKC ThD) can be earned by dogs who have been certified by recognized therapy dog organizations. Visit www.akc.org/akctherapydog.

Index

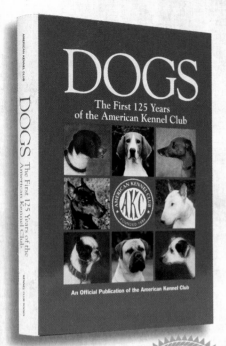

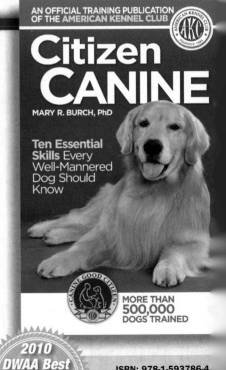

Meet Your Breed

BowTie Press is excited to team up with the American Kennel Club, the most trusted and recognized dog organization in the United States, to launch a new dog breed series, which will be the ultimate resource for family dog care.

AMERICAN KENNEL CLUB

Each title in the series explains what you need to know when raising a purebred dog. From choosing a puppy to feeding and training, the series will encompass life with your dog from beginning to end.

Meet the Boxer
UPC: 7 31360 84745 4
ISBN: 978-1-935484-74-5

Meet the German Shepherd
UPC: 7 31360 84729 4
ISBN: 978-1-935484-72-1

Meet the Lab
UPC: 7 31360 84702 7
ISBN: 978-1-935484-70-7

Meet the Shih Tzu
UPC: 7 31360 84737 9
ISBN: 978-1-935484-73-8

Meet the Yorkie
UPC: 7 31360 84710 2
ISBN: 978-1-935484-71-4

Down-to-earth advice, colorful photos, and a full-length training DVD from the AKC will help dog owners learn how to raise and care for the perfect family companion. This series will help owners raise their puppies every step of the way. As an official publication of the AKC, the books in the series will also include details on dog registration, various AKC programs such as Canine Good Citizen® and S.T.A.R. Puppy®, dog agility, showing, and many other opportunities to get your dog involved with the AKC.

bowtiepress.com

Kennel Club Books®
kennelclubbooks.com

About the Series
$12.95 / $13.95 Can.
Paperback

8 x 11 inches
Full-color photographs
Bonus DVD

AMERICAN KENNEL CLUB®

Advocating for the purebred dog as a family companion, advancing canine health and well-being, working to protect the rights of all dog owners and promoting responsible dog ownership, the **American Kennel Club:**

Sponsors more than **22,000 sanctioned events** annually including conformation, agility, obedience, rally, tracking, lure coursing, earthdog, herding, field trial, hunt test, and coonhound events

Features a **10-step Canine Good Citizen® program** that rewards dogs who have good manners at home and in the community

Has reunited more than **400,000** lost pets with their owners through the AKC Companion Animal Recovery - visit **www.akccar.org**

Created and supports the AKC Canine Health Foundation, which funds research projects using the more than **$22 million** the AKC has donated since 1995 - visit **www.akcchf.org**

Joins **animal lovers** through education, outreach and grant-making via the AKC Humane Fund - visit **www.akchumanefund.org**

We're more than champion dogs. We're the dog's champion.

www.akc.org